Praise for Angelwhispers: Listen for them in your life:

"…Angelwhispers is so inspirational. It has done something to me. Something just wonderful…"

A. G., San Diego, CA

"…I loved your book so much. I am sharing it with friends…"

C. B., Tijeras, NM

"…I have just finished reading your book Angelwhispers and I found it a very enjoyable read. I was very uplifted by it…It is a book that I would pass on and encourage other people to read…"

N. A., Ithaca, NY

"…I was sitting in my living room mourning the death of my son, Tim. I reached down into my end table to find something to read to distract me. I brought up several magazines, puzzles and this book titled Angelwhispers and wondered when I had ordered it. I started to read it and soon learned it was something that I really needed at this time. I cried and thanked the angels and God for such an uplifting message as it was what I really needed to help me through this…"

M. H., Cold Spring, KY

"…I have been surrounded by angels all my life – and know how much comfort they give everyday…I feel sorry for people who don't believe in Angels – they are such a comfort and a joy to have in your life. Thank you for this book…"

S. O., Grants, Pass, OR

"…I just read your story to my daughter and sons and we can't wait to get our hands on Angelwhispers…"

I. W., Dorr, MI

Angelwhispers: Listen for them in your life
By: Marcy D. Nicholas

Published by: Shaw Creative
                PO Box 703
                Uniontown, OH 44685

ISBN: 978-0-9906362-2-9 Paperback
ISBN: 978-0-9906362-1-2 eBook

Library of Congress Cataloging-in Publication Data:
1-1712557341

Printed in the United States of America

2nd Edition
Printing 12 11 10 9 8 7 6 5 4 3 2 1

Angelwhispers:

Listen for them in your life...

by Marcy D. Nicholas

By Maryanne Shaw:

The 9 Week Miracle
http://www.the9weekmiracle.com

The Marcy D. Nicholas Books:

Angel Stories from Across America
Amish Gardening Secrets
The Household Companion
The Food Remedy Handbook
2009 Ways to Live Simply, Smarter, Healthier & Stress Free
The Gardening Book: Tricks, Tips & Secrets of the Trade
Herbs: Nature's Pharmacy or Nature's Poison?
Guide to America's Best Getaways
Natural Home Remedies for Pets

The former Remedy of the Day Daiy Internet Column as well as
these informative booklets:

72 Secrets to Look Younger
Headaches: Is There a Quick Fix?
How to Grow, Dry, Use & Prepare Herbs
Anti-Aging Tips
Use It or Lose It: Home Remedies for your Mind!
Training & Traveling Tips for your Pet
Garlic: Nature's Antibiotic
199 Things Your Mother Used to Tell You
Beware of Identity Theft

Angelwhispers

Angelwhispers. That seemingly insignificant coincidence that isn't a coincidence at all, but rather the angels at work in your life.

From the Author...

Dear Friend,

I don't think it is a coincidence that you are holding this book right now. However it was that you came to be reading it, the messages it contains are meant for you. Since you already have a belief in angels, you aren't going to find a scientific explanation of what angels are and their classifications here. There are plenty of other volumes out there that can do that for you.

This book is different. This one is about *Angelwhispers* – those little coincidences that happen in our lives, those little nudges we get in our minds. They are our angels communicating with us.

You will learn how to open yourself up to recognize these *Angelwhispers* in your daily life and bring about joy, blessings and abundance.

My writing comes from the heart as does my wish for you to hear the *Angelwhispers* in your life.

Kind Regards

Marcy D. Nicholas

Marcy D Nicholas

Table of Contents

Dedication: To Victor & Josephine, who were over my shoulder as I wrote. You have and always will be, my inspiration.

Chapter 1.

Victor's Story:
A Brief History...

Angelwhisper's were always present in Victor's life, and they can be heard in your life if you just stop and listen....

His name was Victor. Throughout all of his 88 years he had believed in angels, and on February 14, 1994 that belief became a reality for his family.

Victor and his wife Josephine had just returned from dinner to celebrate Valentine's Day. Yes, after fifty-five years of marriage, they still celebrated Valentine's Day every year with a nice dinner. That particular year after returning home, they were sitting quietly at the kitchen table. Josephine was watching over him worriedly because Victor was experiencing chest pain. "Just a little pressure", he insisted. "Let's see if it gets better", he said. Josephine anxiously wringing her hands was close to tears. Just then the phone on the wall over her shoulder rang. She answered it and the voice on the other end said "This is 9-1-1, do you have an emergency?" Confused, Josephine could only say "What?" The 911 operator repeated: "This is 9-1-1, do you have an emergency?" Josephine said to Victor, "It's 9-1-1, They want to know if we have an emergency." Victor immediately responded. "That's my angel!

Tell them I need an ambulance!" Josephine then told 9-1-1 that her husband was having chest pain and an ambulance was sent immediately.

What followed was a series of "coincidences" that can only be explained as miraculous. The end result was an 88-year old man having triple bypass heart surgery against great odds. He went on to live six more years. He went on an Alaskan cruise with his wife. He went to Italy with his family. He saw a World Series game. He enjoyed countless family weddings, dinners and get-togethers. Quality of life? In spades! When he finally passed away in 2001, it wasn't his heart that took him.

Victor was my father. I didn't used to be a believer. In fact, I went to the 9-1-1 offices shortly after everything happened to listen to the tape of the 9-1-1 call that night. What I heard was there was no incoming phone call to the 9-1-1 offices...nothing. Just the call from 9-1-1 that my mother answered.

But because of that night and the events that happened since, I know that angels exist. My father wore an angel pin on his lapel every day until the day he died as a reminder, and I have kept angels throughout my home every day since. I will never forget...

Victor's story began long before that cold February day in 1994. He was born September 23, 1906 in East Palestine, Ohio to Italian immigrants James and Elizabeth. He was the second son of what was to be six surviving boys and two girls.

His parents were deeply religious and raised the family with church and God an important part of the family life.

But my dad was a rascal. Back in those days, the only entertainment they had came from their own ingenuity. My dad captured the stories of his boyhood days on a series of tapes that he made. It took him close to a year to complete the many, many stories he told spanning his earliest memories up to include the birth of his children and grandchildren. He would take breaks by ending the sequence on the tape with the words "That's all for now" or "I'll come back later" or even "Till we meet again, so long". I am going to include just a couple of excerpts from *Victor's Story: Until We Meet Again* (This book is slated for publication in 2015).

...On the year 19 and 6, I was born. The date is September the 23rd. I was born in a little town called East Palestine, Ohio, Columbiana County.

...I'll tell you some of the experiences that I had on my first job working in the mine...

...I was supposed to go up one side of the mine to the other. It was called the right and the left. I was going to the right, and I took a short cut to the old workout places. There was swamps in there, water and stuff you know. Here my car light went out. I had no matches. I was left completely in the dark. I said "Oh my God, how in the heck am I gonna get out of here?" Now I remembered what my father said: "If you ever get caught in the mine, just follow the tracks out." So I put my hand on the track and started going, going till I hit a dead end. "Uh oh. I must be

going the wrong way." So I reversed myself and came the other way. I kept going, going, going till my back was almost broken going on all fours you know. And I come around the bend, and I seen a light way to the distance. And I seen that light, and I come out of it. I never told anybody that I got lost. That was really an experience.

...One time my Ma had a dream. In it my dad, who I always called Pop, came home from the mine all bloody. But in the dream she knew he would be okay. The next morning she told Pop about the dream and asked him not to go to work at the mine that day. Of course he didn't listen to her. Later that day while I was working at the mine, I got a telephone call. I used to answer the phone too, you know we had a phone in the mine. The man on the phone said "Hey kid, bring the stretcher up here, somebody got killed up here." So I took the stretcher, and I run up there. I said "Who was it?" He said "No, he didn't get killed, he's badly hurt. Kid, it's your father." Ohhhh my God. I tell you I just went back to my place, took my bucket, and I started going out of the mine. When I came home, they already had put him in an ambulance to the hospital. He had a broken pelvis, broken ribs, cuts and bruises all over. My brother, Herman, had been there at the time. Herman had left to go get a bucket of water. When Pop was loading the clay up under it, the whole coal on top hit the car and broke. Good thing it was wet, it broke up and buried him completely under it. When Herman came up there, he just saw Pop's hand sticking up. Herman scratched and got him out. Oh I wanna tell you, he was a mess...

Both of those excerpts have one common theme. And

that is angels were at work. When my dad lost in the mine, he remembered the words of his father that led to his safety - certainly an *Angelwhisper*. And my grandmother's dream the night before the mine accident, helped prepare her when she received the news that my grandfather had in fact been seriously hurt in the mine. She knew she had received a message from her angels and that he would be ok.

Years later, in 1962, my grandmother had another dream. This one was after the death of her beloved husband, my grandfather. The following day she had planned to pack all of his clothes to give away. In the dream my grandfather told her to cut open the lining of his good coat, and she would find some money. When she awoke, she remembered the dream. She told my dad about it who was 56 years old at the time. Together they went to the closet and retrieved my grandfather's good coat. There was nothing in the pocket. Then my grandmother remembered that in the dream my grandfather said to cut open the lining. When they carefully cut into the lining, they found $300, just as my grandfather said in the dream.

Coincidences?

I don't believe in coincidences. I prefer to call these sometime unbelievable events that happen in all of our lives *Angelwhispers*. In my father's case, here's what happened after he got to the hospital following the 9-1-1 call that I told you about at the beginning of this chapter...

I got the phone call along with my sister and three brothers to go to the hospital. When I walked into my father's hospital room followed by my husband, what I found stopped me in my tracks. The bed was empty and someone from housekeeping was mopping the floor. I stood rooted to the spot, my mind refusing to comprehend the possible meaning. Mean while my husband maneuvered himself behind me, certain I was going to go down. Instead a nurse came in and informed us that my father had been moved and directed us to follow her.

I arrived at his bedside along with the rest of the family. My father was quite animated in the bed, but then, that was dad. He kept saying, *"I'm having a heart attack right now!"* It was only a few minutes later that the cardiologist chased us out with the words, *"We have a lot of work to do"*. That was the beginning of a very long night.

The next morning the news was grim. My father had suffered a heart attack and had sustained damage in over 50% of his heart. He also had three blockages. His long-time family doctor along with the cardiologist concurred in their assessment of the situation. In short their advice was: Go home, sit in a chair and live out the rest of your days quietly. After all Vic, you're 88 years old!

We argued. We cajoled. We pleaded. This was no ordinary 88-year old man. To look at him you would think he was 70 years old tops. He was active, lively and full of pep. To be told to go and live out his days in a chair was devastating to him.

He told the doctors he was willing to have whatever surgery it would take. But when both of these doctors, top men in their field, flatly told him *"No, you're an 88-year old man, surgery is out of the question."* we saw his lower lip quaver and our hearts broke for him. And they wouldn't budge.

And then came *Angelwhisper #2.* The cardiologist was suddenly called out of town and another doctor (I'll call him Dr. Grace) took his place. He came into the hospital to visit my dad. He looked at the chart, looked at the man in the bed, looked at the chart again and asked *"This can't be right, I'm looking for Victor."* My father said, *"I'm Victor."* The doctor was astounded. He later told me *"I went into that room looking for an 88-year old man and I knew when I saw your father that wasn't him!"*

Anyway after familiarizing himself with his case, Dr Grace called the family together to have a discussion. He said he felt our father was unlike the typical 88-year old man and would benefit from open-heart surgery if we would consider it. We were ecstatic! But we cautioned, you'll never convince our family doctor. At this Dr Grace said, *"Your family doctor just left on vacation, so there is another doctor covering for him. I know him pretty well, and I think he'll agree with me".* *Angelwhisper #3.*

Well, he was right. Both doctors agreed and presented the case to one of the leading heart surgeons in the nation who practiced at a hospital about an hour from our home. He agreed to do the surgery!

I stayed with my mother during the first forty-eight critical hours following the surgery in a suite of rooms especially reserved for patient's families. Dr Grace stayed in touch throughout, answering questions and helping us through the process.

My father made a splendid recovery. The two original doctors were none too pleased when they both returned. One of the first things we did was to change doctors. The two new doctors who walked into our lives just when they were needed faded away, and I've never seen them again. I've tried to find Dr. Grace, but have never been successful.

So yes, dad did go on for six more years after that surgery. Six full, loving, life-filled years. During that time I was privileged to accompany my parents to Italy where we visited both of the home towns of their parents. We met many, many relatives and ate lots of wonderful food. I could fill many pages with the story of that trip.

His favorite baseball team was always the Cleveland Indians. When my brother took him to a World Series game, I think his smile lit up the entire ballpark.

He had experienced high quality of life through the better part of those six years when he peacefully passed away at the age of 94 surrounded by his family. He had an angel pin on the lapel of his pajamas the day he died, just as he wore on each day of the six years. He never forgot. And neither did I.

Chapter 2.

Angels Around Us

A genuine encounter with a holy angel will glorify God, not the angel. Holy angels never draw attention to themselves. They typically do their work and disappear.

The Gift of Angels[1]

Our angels are all around us. Some of us are more attuned to this than others. If you are reading this, my guess is you fall into this category.

Even though I was raised Catholic, went to twelve years of catholic schools, spent a lot of hours listening to my dad talk about God and the angels, I know that I missed many *Angelwhispers* in my younger years.

Being raised Catholic, we were taught about our Guardian Angels. As a child, I always pictured in my mind this gentle being walking beside me, protecting me from tripping, falling or other dangers. A lot of what I pictured in my mind came from drawings of angels I had seen in books. The angels were always beautiful with large wings wearing flowing white gowns.

Later I pictured my angel riding alongside me in the

---

1   *The Gift of Angels: Inspirational Encounters with God's Heavenly Messengers,* 2003 by Zondervan, Grand Rapids, MI, Compiler: Rebecca Currington in conjunction with Snapdragon Editorial Group Inc.

car or holding my hand in times of need. I always talked to my children about angels, making them aware of their own Guardian Angels in their lives.

When I was a child I thought everyone had one Guardian Angel. Now I believe we can have more than one.

I'd like to share a story with you of an experience my grandson had with his Guardian Angel when he was only sixteen months old.

My daughter lived in a small town about ninety minutes from me alone with her sixteen month old son, Clayton. She called me one morning totally distraught because she had taken Clayton to the doctor. He had been sick and was getting worse. The doctor said he had a bad case of pneumonia. They sent him home with medicine and instructions for breathing treatments every hour. She was to return in the morning and at that time they would most likely have to hospitalize him and put IV's into his head. My daughter was practically incoherent. I calmed her down as best I could, reminding her to be strong for the baby, and told her I would leave immediately to be with the two of them.

I arrived to find a very sick little boy. Throughout the day his mother lovingly applied the breathing treatments as instructed to a very unwilling participant. In between, little Clayton was happy to have both his mother and I there.

Late that evening, my daughter was sitting on the couch

and Clayton was resting on her lap. I was sitting on a chair to the side of them. Suddenly Clayton lifted his head and pointed to a spot over my head and said "Angel!" He kept his head up and again pointed and said "Angel!" My daughter and I both knew that Clayton knew exactly what angels were and she immediately got scared and a bit emotional and said "Oh my God!" I on the other hand was overjoyed! I said "Don't be afraid! He is seeing his Guardian Angel. That means he is going to be OK!"

Clayton kept his head in an upright position for a little while longer, while still in a reclining position on the couch, all the while never taking his eyes off that point above my head. Finally he slowly lowered his head back down and he stayed quiet.

The next morning, my daughter tried to justify what she had seen and heard. She said, "He really didn't see an angel. He was pointing to this". By "this" she was referring to a porcelain baby figurine I had given her, dressed in a white lace gown with a halo over its head that she had hanging on the knob of the curio cabinet that had been behind me. I knew better but I had to prove it.

So a while later I took Clayton into my daughter's bedroom. I pointed to an angel figurine and said "What's that?" Clayton said "Angel!" I walked over to another angel figurine and said "What's that?" Clayton said "Angel!" I walked over to the baby figurine and said "What's that?" Clayton just looked at it and didn't answer as if to say "I don't know, what is it?"

I think that proved my point, he was not looking at that baby figurine the night before. I believe in my heart he saw his Guardian Angel.

My daughter and I returned to the doctor that next morning with Clayton and the doctor was astounded at Clayton's improvement. The doctor told her he was sure that when she returned with Clayton that morning he would have to be admitted into the hospital. My daughter and I just looked at each other. We were both remembering the events of the night before - and Clayton's Angel.

> *Why is it that angels like disguise? It seems they take whatever form the visited person is willing to accept; and sometimes no form at all – a dream, a thought a surge of power, a sense of guidance...*[2]

Do you ever get little premonitions? I'm talking about sudden urges to suddenly stop at a certain store or drive a different route home. Sometimes seemingly crazy ideas will pop into your head for unknown reasons. An example might be to put a weird item into your car. Another might be to take an item out of storage and put it where it is readily accessible. You may get the urge to buy some obscure item you haven't thought of in years. Don't ignore these little intuitions. They are nudges from your angel.

Back in November of 2000, we were on a business trip out west in our motorhome. This is an excerpt from my journal from that trip:

---

2   *A Book of Angels by Sophy Burnham,* 1990, 2004 by Sophy Burnham. A Ballantine Book Published by The Random House Publishers Group New York.

(While driving through Missouri on I-44W)… It started raining about 10 AM, and rained off and on. About 12:30 we were at a complete standstill. The reason became clear soon. A car and a pickup truck were off the road in the grass to the right. They must have skidded on the wet roads. The thing is, the accident had happened only shortly before. We had decided to stop, spur-of-the-moment to top off our gas tank and get coffee, then I walked over to an adjoining gift shop to buy a paper. If we hadn't, we could have been involved. Thank you Lord!

Intuition is …the "still small voice" commonly called a hunch, which says, "this is the way, walk ye in it".[3]

Research gives you knowledge
Knowledge gives you confidence
Confidence conquers fear[4]

I read a lot. So I can't tell you where I read this specific story. But there was a doctor who attended a medical conference. He was ready to leave then, at the last minute he decided to stay and attend one more seminar about an obscure medical procedure. The very next day after he returned to his own hospital, an emergency patient was brought in needing that very procedure he just learned about. Angelwhisper maybe?

There are many examples similar to these next two that you have probably heard time and time again. They are about

---

3   *The Power of the Spoken Word,* 2007 by Florence Scovel Shinn, Wilder Publications, Radford, VI.
4   *Changing Your Course the 5 Step Guide to Getting the Life You Want,* Bob & Melinda Blanchard. 2008, Sterling Publishing Co Inc. New York, NY.

being in the right place at the right time. *Or are they?*

A man is at a convenience store. Suddenly, he slumps to the floor from an apparent heart attack. Another shopper recognized what was happening and immediately starts cardiopulmonary resuscitation (CPR). When the paramedics arrive, they say this man's quick thinking is what saved his life. When interviewed, the man says he was headed home and spur of the moment stopped in for a cup of coffee. He'd never been in that convenience store before.

A woman was helping her friend at her garage sale. They were eating lunch when suddenly she chokes on a french fry. She can't dislodge the food. A man who was browsing quickly goes over and does the Heimlich maneuver. Afterwards he said he saw the sign for the sale because he took a route he doesn't usually take. Thus he turned down the street and saw the garage sale sign and decided to stop.

Both of these examples were people who listened to their angel nudges. They were voices in their heads that said something, like in the second case *"Turn here! You just want to Turn here!"* He must have listened because he showed up at that garage sale.

In the first case, the conversation may have sounded like this *"You want coffee, look for a convenience store. You need coffee. No, not that store, the next one. Coffee, coffee, coffee. Ummmmm, Can't you smell it? Get ready to turn up ahead. Yes, you want to stop at the convenience store at the next light for coffee".*

If he was anything like me at first, I resisted and tried to argue with my inner urgings. There was in fact a time when I had this inner dialogue and an instinct to stop for coffee and I ignored it. This was before my "blanket" experience below. Who knows what person I was supposed to meet and perhaps help?

One cold December evening when my children were very little, we had gone to spend the evening with friends. Before we left, I had the weird thought pop into my head to put some blankets into the car. I thought that was odd as it was 45 degrees outside and we were only going 25 minutes away, so I pushed it aside. Again and again the thought would pop into my head. Each time I would think, "Why on earth am I thinking that?" And each time, I would push the thought out of my mind.

We left that evening with my nine-month old son, four year-old son and seven year old daughter and had a nice evening with our friends. When we left to go home, it was after midnight. The temperature had plummeted almost forty degrees, and with the wind chill we were talking sub-zero.

On the way home, our car broke down in that frigid air. We were in a rural area, and the few houses around all were dark. My baby began to cry and my older children were scared. I tried to keep them calm by having them recite with me the *Hail Mary*. My husband went to the nearest farmhouse and *God Bless* the woman who lived there. She opened her door to our family, and let us use her phone. You have to remember that this was way before cell phones. She gave us a warm place to sit and wait. We got my brother, Vic, out of bed, and he came and got us and took us home. Our car stayed by the side of the road overnight. Ever since that night, when I drive past that house I silently bless that woman for her kindness. How many would open the door to a strange man at that hour of the night? Remember I was in the car with my children. All she saw at her door was a man. I think maybe *she* was an angel.

Ever since that night when I didn't put those blankets in my car, I have listened to those voices in my head.

> *Trust in yourself. Your perceptions are often far more accurate than you are willing to believe.*[5]

Here's another journal excerpt from the western trip:

> (Still on I-44W.) The long travel day got even longer as we approached Flagstaff, and the sky started to look stormy. It sprinkled, then it rained, then it iced, then it snowed, and I mean snowed! I wanted to stop in Flagstaff and camp, but Skip said no, who knew how bad it was gonna get; we could get stuck there. He was right, but I was so scared. We got off I-40W and onto Route 17S, and it was snowing like crazy. After a while it changed to rain. We needed gas, so we stopped at

---

5   *Quote:* Claudia Black.

Meads Park. There was a campground there I wanted to stay in, but it was also 7000´ elevation and the snow was coming. The lady there I paid for the gas said our destination, Sedona, would be fine. So we headed in. When we turned off Route 17S onto Route 179, it was about 15 miles in. It wasn't a bad road, (89A would have been all switchbacks) but there were grades; and it was dark and raining. I was nervous about missing our turn in the dark and rain. (Remember when you are 35´ long pulling a car, you can't just turn around easily!) But we pulled over a few times, and with me standing with my nose to the windshield we finally found the turn and the campground.

The office was closed when we got in, but they had a map for us taped to the door with our site marked. Skip unhooked the car and I led the way to the campsite. Then he went to back into the site, and we had no reverse! There we were in the pouring down rain, and we didn't know what to do. Skip shut the engine off, Then he had me get in and try it. I got behind the wheel, said a quick prayer to St Jude, and lo and behold we had reverse! Skip talked me through it, and I backed in. Then I sat and cried. Thank you Lord for keeping us safe today...

Think of incidents that have happened in your life. Sometimes they are so unobtrusive that you can miss them very easily. We tend to think it is all in our own mind, our own mindless chatter. But that is not the case.

Be still, and be attentive. When something strikes you, that is what God wants to talk to you about. Sometimes it's an image, sometimes it's a thought or a word. Listen for it. Open up, shut out the noise. Wait for it. Put away the distractions. You'll feel it in your gut.

Prayers don't have to be formal. Just talk to God and your angels. They listen and hear you. Here is a prayer I found I had written in one of my journals:

Thank you for the joy of my angels. I feel them all around me, and miss them every day. Oh that I could be like them and make them proud! Oh Lord hear my prayer.

Upon re-reading the above words in the context of when it was written, I believe I was speaking about my deceased parents as my angels. Technically loved ones who go before us are not angels but rather spirit guides. But that goes beyond the scope of this book. If it comforts you, as it did me, to refer to them in that way, you certainly aren't hurting anyone. I can't help but to associate "angels" with my mother and father.

A couple of years ago I had to have back surgery. One night during my recovery, I couldn't sleep. This is an excerpt from my journal:

> I took a pill around 10PM and fell asleep at 11:30. I woke at 2:30 and read but was still awake at 6:30. I was so dead tired, but couldn't sleep. So I decided to pray. I had been reading *90 Minutes in Heaven* by Don Piper and

remembered when frustrated to pray to God. I thought to myself "Praise the Lord! The Lord is my Shepherd!" and fell asleep – that quickly. A few minutes later, Skip came into the bedroom and started talking to me thinking I was awake. I woke up and was frustrated he woke me up. Then I told him it was OK, and I repeated my prayers of peace. Seconds later I was asleep, and I slept soundly for 3 1/2 hours.

Always be aware of how you feel. If you feel hopeless, that isn't from God. Go back to your center, the place of hope, and get centered again. Life is about rediscovery. Each time we will grow more confident. When you have a decision to make, go inside before you decide. That is where we get clarity. Being quiet and hearing God inside of us helps us have a clearer mind to what is the right decision. Recognize when you are being pulled away from the truth. So pay attention and center yourself again. The more we come to know God, the more we come to know ourselves. Sometimes that means letting go of something we've known for a long time. What is true will bring you peace. Pay attention to people around you, when reading the paper, watching the news. He will call you when he wants you to act. The message will be there. Pay attention.

Sometimes the "nudges" come in other forms. They may be a song that you keep hearing over and over again, and the message is in the lyrics. Maybe it is a stranger's conversation that you overhear. Sometimes it is someone from your past that has been on your mind, and then you bump into them. This is not a coincidence. This accidental meeting happens because one of you has a message for the other.

Change

You must believe that you can make life-changing choices in order to transform your dreams into specific goals. Otherwise, your life will end up as a chain of events that happen because of other people's decisions, not your own. Someone else will be running your life.[6]

Change occurs when one becomes what she is, not when she tries to become what she is not.[7]

Let's face it, change can be scary. Change can also be exhilarating. Some of us are more adaptable to change than others. If you've ever worked with people, you know exactly what I mean. A perfect example is working in an

---

6   *Changing Your Course the 5 Step Guide to Getting the Life You Want,* Bob & Melinda Blanchard. 2008, Sterling Publishing Co Inc. New York, NY.

7   *Quote:* Ruth P. Freedman. Paper: *The Paradoxical Theory of Change,* Arnold Beisser, 1970.

office transitioning a new computer system. The ones who aren't adaptable to change are always saying things like "It won't do it!" or "We used to be able to do it like this!" and the inevitable "This is stupid!" Oh, they will finally learn it, but they will never own up to their mistakes. It will always be the computer's fault, the company's fault for switching systems, the trainer's fault for not telling them a key point and so on. Their attitude is poor and if layoffs have to occur, they wonder why they are first on the list.

On the flip side, the ones who are adaptable seem to be sailing right through. The bottom line is they have a good attitude. They embrace the present moment and accept life as it is. This just makes the whole process easier.

Let's apply this scenario to our lives. We are working in a job we are comfortable with, our home life is stable. Then all of a sudden, everything changes.

Whether it be a transfer, loss of job due to downsizing, layoff or termination, each of these bring their own unique mental shifts and possible financial hardship. And change.

Whether it be a marriage, separation, divorce or death, each brings differences in the home life as we had known. And change.

My husband and I were in a situation such as I described, comfortable in our jobs and home life. Suddenly the rug was pulled from under us when he was let go from his job with no warning. We were both shellshocked. After dusting himself off, he immediately got to work putting the word out that he was available. Within five days, he was brought onboard at another facility. Not only did this seem to be a better opportunity at the time but it has proven itself now five years later. Had he not lost his job, this couldn't have happened. Things do happen for the better good. We just have to be patient for it to play out.

I know being patient is hard. I also know accepting life's tough curve balls is hard too. I'm not trying to say it is easy to just accept whatever hardship you happen to be dealing with right now or change you happen to be going through. But you have two choices. Accept it or Not. If you don't accept it, will it go away? I think you know the answer to that one. By fighting it, your life will just be harder.

By accepting it and praying to God to help you, it will make your cross easier to bear. Ask your angels to help you. There are ways to find answers. Trust me, it works.

> *Everyone has a path to walk that will help someone he or she loves to do more, be more and learn more, so that person in turn can pass it on to future loved ones who will do the same, and so on.*[8]

> *Most of our stress and suffering comes not from events, but from our thoughts. Reframe negative thoughts, and stress subsides.*[9]

> *If you want others to be happy, practice compassion. If you want to be happy, practice compassion.*[10]

We also must be alert not to compare ourselves to others. Their success is not our failure! I know it is part of human nature to compete, but let's keep that within the sports arena or other like competitions and out of the game of life. I also know that can be easier said than done.

Let's take for example three women involved in direct

---

8   Martha Beck, PH.D., Life Coach. *Secrets of the Monarch, Allison O. DuBois,* 2007 by Allison DuBois, Published by Fireside Books, a divison of Simon & Schuster Inc.

9   Martha Beck, PH.D., Life Coach. *We Empower,* Maria Shriver 2008 California Governor and First Lady's Conference on Women, New York, NY

10 *The Art of Happiness, A Handbook for Living,* 1998 by His Holiness Dalai Lama & Howard C. Cutler M.D., Riverhead Books, Published by the Penguin Group, New York, NY.

sales. I'll call them Tess, Suzie and Amy. Tess has a full time job and a four-year old son. She works her direct sales business part time and makes sure she spends at least one half hour per day on lunch hours and evenings doing something to promote her business, phone calls, addressing invitations or other quick duties. She uses the time in the nooks and crannies of her life to get things done. Her average sales for the month are consistently $1500.

Suzie works her direct sales business full time and has no children. Her average sales for the month are consistently $7000.

Amy has a full time job and a twelve-year old daughter. She works her direct sales business part time. She has inconsistent sales ranging from $400 to $700 per month. There are even months with zero sales.

Every month Tess listens to the recognition and hears Suzie's numbers and feels she isn't as good. She wracks her brain to try to come up with ways to get more time out of her day so she can stack up better against Suzie. She is dejected.

Every month Amy hears the same numbers and thinks Suzie sells so much because she doesn't work. She justifies to herself that she doesn't have time to work her business during the day, and at night sometimes she is just too tired and would rather just lie on the couch and watch TV. She is irritated.

Do you see what is wrong with both Tess and Amy's

thinking? Tess is comparing herself to Suzie and not giving herself any credit at all. Amy is making excuses for her own behavior and refuses to face the truth about her own laziness.

An important lesson for all of us is that we should never compare ourselves to anybody. Each of our lives are unique. We have our own circumstances to deal with. With that being said, as long as you are honestly doing everything that you can do to make the best use of your time, you can ask no more of yourself. But you must be honest with yourself. Brutally honest.

It doesn't serve us well to look upon others good fortune, accomplishments and abilities with envy or disdain. Always bless the good achievements of others, and those blessings will come back to you. Sometimes we may find this difficult. That's because we're human. If so, just say a simple prayer, and ask your angels to help you.

What about when bad luck falls on someone we dislike or who has wronged us? I strongly believe that what goes around comes around. I have gotten through some difficult times with difficult people by telling myself those words. Try to refrain from having any joy in their hard luck. Instead send them a silent blessing. You will be blessed all the more for it.

Bless someone else's day with small acts of kindness. Make a visit. Phone someone who may be lonely just to chat. Smile. Sometimes the smallest of actions make the biggest difference.

Free Will

We all have free will. When we get the little "nudges" from our angels, we have the free will to take the guidance and follow what they are trying to do for us - or not. Like when I should have put the blankets in the car.

Have you even gotten an idea for what you think is the greatest invention in the world? I'm sure you have. But did you act on it? Probably not. Then years later, I'll bet "your" invention came out on the market. Did you say something like, "That's my invention"! Well, it might have been, had you acted on it. I believe those little ideas come from our angels. Then if we don't act on them, they give them to someone else until eventually the idea comes to fruition.

Many, many years ago I had an idea for a windshield wiper for the rear window of cars. At that time it was unheard of, and I thought that would be a grand idea. Apparently it was, as now most cars are equipped with them. Should have acted on it.

My point is we cannot be smug enough to think that we

are the only one in the universe that gets that one unique idea. Or that when we do get an inspired idea that we can just sit on it. We get inspired ideas for a reason. *And that reason is to do something with them.*

And what about the tragedies that happen in life? Why does God let them happen? It is because God does not intervene with free will. As hard as it is for us to accept why some of the horrible things happen in our world, it is not for us to understand the whys. We just have to have faith that God loves us and that there is a reason for the greater good. There is a purpose, and it isn't our place as humans to question nor understand exactly how it all fits together. We just have to have faith and stay close to God. Live a good life, and it will all work out in the end.

Chapter Suggestions:

- Keep a journal of your angel "nudges". Write them down at the end of the day, early morning or whatever time works best for you. It should be when you have some quiet time, and it doesn't have to be a big block of time either.

- These "nudges" often include dreams as often we can get answers or ideas to worries we are carrying around with us in our dreams. Take a few minutes in the morning when you wake up to try to remember your dreams before you start to think about all you have to do in the day ahead. Dreams can be fragile. If you bombard your mind with details of life, you can lose the fragments of your dreams. But if you take those few minutes while you are still between sleep and wakefulness, you may be surprised at what you recollect.

- Write down your inspired ideas. Especially take note of things that come to you repeatedly and take action!

Chapter 3.

Seeking Guidance: Communication with your Angels

All you need to do to receive guidance is to ask for it and then listen[11]

> *The more faithfully you listen to the voice within you, the better you will hear what is sounding outside. And only she who listens can speak.*
> Dag Hammarskjold

We don't have all the answers. While some of us may think that we do, the fact is, we don't. We all need help and guidance along life's path. We especially need it in times of turmoil. Our angels are always around us. When we pray to God, often he sends his angels into our lives to help us. We just don't realize it.

To prepare for communicating with your angel, always have pen and paper handy to write down any thoughts that come to mind. Remember, it's for your eyes only. Put the date at the top. I like to use a journal especially for this purpose that I call *Angel Conversations,* then I just record the dates. If there are any questions you have, write them down ahead

---

11   *Sould Love, Awakening Your Heart Centers,* 1997 by Sanaya Roman, HJ Kramer Inc., Tiburon, CA.

of time. Keep them simple and with no negative connotation. Always ask honest questions from your heart. For example, *"Is there something you can tell me right now about _____?"* or "What changes should I make in my life right now?" I always begin the entry with a *"Welcome"* and I ask for their name, then I end the entry with a "Thank You" as a symbol of gratitude. I also can't stress enough not to judge what thoughts pop into your mind. Just write them down!

You may be wondering, "How do I know if the words that pop into my mind come from my angel and not from my own mind?" The best answer I can give you is your angel will never say anything negative or judgmental. Guidance from your angel will give you a warm and fuzzy feeling. Even if you are being warned of trouble, you will feel loved and cared for. Any answers or inspiration you get come to you suddenly. And the angels will speak to you in the second person, such as "You should turn left up ahead" or "You should apply for a consolidation loan".

Your mind will also always speak to you in the first person, such as "I should turn left at the next light" or "I should apply for a bank loan". Communication coming from your own mind will be connected to feelings of fear and unworthiness, a sort of coldness and won't be consistent. It may also tend to procrastinate. We won't hear our angels speak to us if we are distracted or if we don't want to hear what they have to say.

You can be sure that it is your own mind if when during

the process of trying to communicate with your angel you experience thoughts such as "This is boring" or "It's not working". Negative thoughts such as this are judgmental and should be gently pushed away with a prayer to your angel to help you.

Trust your emotions, your feeling and your senses. Pray for an open mind to hear the truth and just trust.

Steps for Communicating with your Angel:

1. To learn to communicate with your angels, the first thing you have to do is have faith and be willing to trust. Clear away the negative emotions toward yourself and others.
2. Make sure you are alone where you have some quiet, uninterrupted time. Silence the phones and other distractions.
3. You'll want to find a place in your home to use for meditation. It doesn't have to be an entire room, it can be just a corner. Some create an altar with religious articles including an angel and candles. Others choose an area that just feels right for them. You'll know the right spot.
4. Always start with a prayer. Ask God and the angels for protection. Visualize a white light around the entire room. This represents God's love and protection.
5. If desired, play soft music of an inspiring or uplifting nature during your mediation time.

6. Relax and get comfortable. Concentrate on relaxing each part of your body. Close your eyes, clearing your mind of all the chatter.

7. Breathe slowly in, then exhale and visualize white light surrounding you.

8. As you breathe, visualize the white light seeping into your feet and slowly working its way up your legs, first into your ankles, then your calves, then up to your knees, your thighs, your hips, your stomach. Feel the warmth. If your mind wanders, pull it back gently and concentrate on your breathing as you feel the energy of the white light as it spreads up your back across your shoulders, down your arms, into your hands. The warmth spreads into your neck and into your face and head. You feel the warmth of the energy throughout your entire body. Your senses are awake and you are listening.

9. Visualize your angels around you.

10. Open your eyes to write down any thoughts that come to you regardless of what they are. Don't try to analyze them, just write them down. Some people may get strong feelings and thoughts. Write these down too. You may notice scents or hear music, write these down. If you see anything visually, write it down.

11. If at any point you feel the need to get re-centered, visualize a cloud floating in the sky. Imagine you are on the cloud floating aimlessly. Feel the warmth of energy as you breathe slowly in and out. Listen.

12. As you get more comfortable with listening to your angel messages and writing them down, you may be

able to ask questions throughout your mediation. If so, just write down the question and answer as it pops into your mind. Remember – no judgments!

13. Before you end your session, be sure to thank your angel with a sincere heart. Ask for all things for the greater good. Gratitude is the most important step when asking for help.

There is enough true abundance for all of us, and God wants it for everyone. So when you pray, always add the words "for the greater good" to your prayer.

Meditation is concentrated focus...The same kind of focus can be accomplished while we paint, garden, write, sing, act, dance, work, exercise, etc. Whenever we tune it to the creative force within ourselves, we are in essence meditating.[12]

Always have gratitude for the present moment as gratitude and the fullness of life now is true prosperity. It can't come in the future. Then in time, that prosperity manifests for you in various ways.[13]

There are ways that our departed loved ones let us know they are around. Have you noticed things like...

---

12 *Talking to Heaven, James VanPraagh,* 1997 by James VanPraagh. The Penguin Group, NY.

13 *Talking to Heaven, James VanPraagh,* 1997 by James VanPraagh. The Penguin Group, NY.

Lights: Flickering, new bulbs burn out instantly.

Television: Scrambled pictures, turning off and on by itself at strange hours or odd times of the day.

Radios: Clock radio at bedside turning on at different hours, could be at hour of significance, Turning on to a significant song.

Music: In their own way, spirits can impress you with a song or you may think of them when a song is played on the radio.

Clocks: Stops at the exact moment a loved one passed, clock or watch stops working for no reason.

Appliances: Stop and start, common when the spirit was very involved with cooking or spent a lot of time in the kitchen.

Smells: Cigar, perfume, roses. Suddenly infiltrates the room. This lets us know they are nearby.

Animals: Spirits can influence a bird or small animal to come by us to get our attention in some way. It's another sign of their nearness to us.

Show me the path where I should walk, Oh Lord; point out the right road for me to follow. [14]

---

14   *The Holy Bible,* Psalm 25:4.

Specific Intentions

Regardless of your intention, whatever it is that you
desire in your life, when asking for it you must pray for it as
though you have already received it. Don't try to figure out
how it will happen. That isn't for you to worry about. This is
where trust in God and the universe to provide comes in. Your
prayer must always, always include the element of gratitude.
Also, what you need, you must give. That is very powerful.
If you need money, give money. If you need time, give time.
Giving indicates that you have plenty and it is a powerful
action that will bring more of the same back into your life.

Now please do not misunderstand me here. I am not
suggesting that you not pay your mortgage payment so you
can give money to help the needy. Nor am I saying that you
should take off work to volunteer. Use common sense. But
giving where it hurts is a very powerful thing.

My brother, Jim, was once having a slow period in his
business. He was visiting a monastery when a monk there
admired the pea coat he was wearing and commented he'd
once been in the Navy. Jim could tell the monk really liked the
coat. In fact, Jim really loved the coat too. He offered it to the
monk anyway. But the monk refused to take it. So Jim asked to
trade him for his *Fruit of the Loom*™ hoodie. Happily the monk
agreed, and the trade was made. Jim saw him softly caressing
the coat and got a warm feeling inside in spite of the cold air
seeping inside of his newly donned hoodie. Right after that,
his business hit on a million-dollar product and soared. An

Angelwhisper for sure.

When giving, always give without expecting payment in return. Give quietly without expecting recognition. Keep it between you and God. Do good deed without telling anyone you did them. Try to do something nice for someone every day, even if it is just holding a door open for someone or letting someone go ahead of you in line.

Be generous with your time. All of us can spare more than we think we can. Think of someone who is lonely and go visit them. Even if you stayed just fifteen minutes, you will have brightened their entire week. If you are short on time and you give time, you may be surprised at how time suddenly opens up for you. With God all things are possible.

What you think about, you bring about.[15]

One receives only that which is given. The game of life is a game of boomerangs. Our thoughts, deeds and words, return to us sooner or later, with astounding accuracy.[16]

Abundance

Sample prayer: *I am grateful for what I have. I have money overflowing. There is an abundance of money and it's on its way to me all for the greater good. Thank you for all of the blessings in my life.*

---

15   *Secrets of the Monarch, Allison O. DuBois,* 2007 by Allison DuBois, Published by Fireside Books, a divison of Simon & Schuster Inc.
16   *The Power of the Spoken Word,* 2007 by Florence Scovel Shinn, Wilder Publications, Radford, VI.

Visualize opening envelopes full of cash or envelopes full of checks all made out to you. ***Don't*** think about bills and not having enough or you will get more of the same. ***Don't*** think *"This stuff doesn't work."* because if you do, the Universe says, *"Your wish is my command"*, and your potential for abundance disappears.[17]

> *The process of incorporating practical praying into your routine may not bring you wealth, but it might very well bring you something more important – abundance… in all areas.*[18]

Anger

Sample prayer: *Dear God make me an instrument of thy love. I want to be like you. I have forgiven them, and I have forgiven myself.*

> *How can we expect God to hear our request when we have hatred in our heart? We must approach God for guidance by sincerely forgiving and filling our hearts with love and forgiveness toward anyone who we believe has wronged us.*[19]

Visualize happy times when you are feeling angry or sad. This changes the negative vibration to a positive one. ***Don't*** allow

---

17   *The Secret,* Rhonda Byrne, 2006 by TS Production Limited Liability Company, Beyond Words Publishing, Hillsboro, OR.

18   *Practical Praying,* John Edward, 2005 by John Edward Princess Books, NY.

19   *Inspiration: Your Ultimate Calling,* Dr Wayne W. Dyer, 2006 by Wayne Dyer, Hay House Inc., Carlsbad, CA.

your mind to remind you of what caused you to be angry in the first place. Gently push the thoughts away and repeat your prayer. Remember you cannot harm others with unkind thoughts, you only harm yourself. All of those thoughts reflect back on you and bring those trials into your own life.

Relationships

Sample prayer: *I am grateful for what I have. I am filled with joy and love. I cherish the soulmate who is on its way to me. Thank you for the blessings in my life.*

Visualize scenarios focusing on the good aspects of your partner's personality. **Don't** focus on the bad qualities or those are the ones that will shine through.

*If you are looking for a relationship, visualize a faceless person in these scenarios. Set an extra place at the dinner table for them each night to symbolize you are ready to welcome them into your life. Park your car to one side of the garage to make room. Sleep on one side of the bed. Make closet space.

Health

Sample prayer: *I am grateful for all that I have. I am vibrant and healthy and feel good. There is joy in living in every fiber of my being. Thank you for all the blessings in my life.*

Visualize doing everything you want to do. Push thoughts

away that say you can't do things because of your illness. Concentrate on the positive. **Don't** talk about your ailments or you are inviting more of the same. Put your energies to feelings of health.

*It is hard for us sometimes to accept when a loved one has to suffer with a serious illness. But we have to remember that each of us has a purpose to fulfill on this earth; and when that purpose has been completed, we will leave. Although we may not understand the why's, there is a reason for everything. As humans we won't ever understand, we just have to have faith that there is a reason. Refer to the end of Chapter 5, and read *Life's Weaving*. I've always gotten comfort from it. I hope you will too.

> *The bottom line is that I am responsible for my own well-being, my own happiness. The choices and decisions I make regarding my life directly influence the quality of my days.*[20]

Events from the Past

If you find yourself constantly talking about events that happened in the past and still getting angry, sad or melancholy, STOP! All you are doing is bringing more difficult circumstances into your present life. You must let it go. No matter what it was. You have to concentrate on now, this minute and go forward.

---

20   *Quote,* Kathleen Andrus, Bestinspiration.com.

Sample prayer: *I am grateful for what I have. Help me to let the past go and concentrate on my present. Fill my heart with your love and forgiveness so I can do this all for the greater good. Thank you for all the blessings in my life.*

Visualize a great weight lifting off your shoulders and your heart feeling lighter and your body buoyed by the feeling. Allow the feeling of joy to spread throughout your entire body. Don't be disappointed if the transformation doesn't happen overnight. It may have taken a lifetime for you to live in the past, the change may not occur overnight. Just continue to ask your angels for help. **Don't** allow the negative thoughts and emotions to crowd in reminding you of the past hurts. Gently push them away and repeat your prayer.

> *Everyone visualizes whether he knows it or not. Visualizing is the great secret of success.*[21]

The Saints and Your Intentions

Saint Anthony - The patron saint of lost items. When you see artwork of St Anthony of Padua, he is wearing a brown Franciscan robe and is usually holding the Christ child and a lily. He is most well known for being the patron saint of lost articles. Belief is very powerful. I can't tell you how many times lost items have just appeared by my just praying to St Anthony for his assistance in locating them.

Saint Christopher – The patron saint of travelers. Officially

---

21   *Your Invisible Power,* 1980 by Genevieve Behrend (1881-1960), Devorss & Co., Camarillo, CA.

St Christopher is not listed any longer as a patron saint as the story is considered to be based on legend. However many still consider having St Christopher medals and pins the best thing to have along on a journey as they still look to St Christopher as the patron saint of travelers.

Saint Francis of Assisi – Patron Saint of Animals. When you see artwork of St Francis of Assisi he is wearing a brown Franciscan robe and is surrounded by animals. Well known for writing the Prayer of St Francis, we used to sing the hymn version when I was in high school:

> *Make me a channel of your peace,*
> *Where there is hatred let me bring your love,*
> *Where there is injury your pardon Lord,*
> *And where there's doubt true faith in you.*
> *Make me a channel of your peace,*
> *Where there's despair in life, let me bring hope,*
> *Where there is darkness, only light,*
> *And where there's sadness, ever joy.*
> *O Master grant that I may never seek,*
> *So much to be consoled as to console,*
> *To be understood as to understand,*
> *To be loved as to love with all my soul.*
> *Make me a channel of your peace,*
> *It is in pardoning that we are pardoned,*
> *In giving to all men that we receive*
> *And in dying that we are born to eternal life.*[22]

Saint Joseph - The husband of the Virgin Mary and a skilled

---

22   *Make Me A Channel of Your Peace,* Royal British Legion.

carpenter. Best known for his assistance in real estate transactions.

It does make sense that St Joseph is the patron saint of homes since he was the guardian of the holiest of families of all mankind. If you need some assistance selling your home, St Joseph can help!

Here's how it works:

1. Buy a statue of St Joseph. Since you are supposed to display the statue somewhere in your new home after your house sells, choose carefully. If you prefer, you can buy a ready-made kit that includes a small plastic statue.
2. Bury the statue with prayerful intentions. Ask for God's guidance as you pray for your needs. Ask that the new buyers be happy there. Instructions say he should be buried upside down and facing the street, though I'm not sure this really matters as long as your intentions are genuine and prayerful. According to Stephen J Binz, author of *St Joseph, My Real Estate Agent,* the gesture of burying the statue upside down is a symbolic, even humorous gesture. It indicates that the burial is temporary and soon to be made right as you honor the statue in your new home.
3. After the house sells, remove the statue and place it proudly somewhere in your new home.[14]

There are countless stories of the wonders of this faith-filled devotion helping thousands!

Saint Jude - Patron Saint of Desperate Situations.

Prayer to St Jude: Most holy apostle, St Jude, faithful servant and friend of Jesus, the Church honors and invokes you universally, as the patron of hopeless cases, of things almost despaired of. Pray for me, I am so helpless and alone. Make use I implore you, of that particular privilege given to you, to bring visible and speedy help where help is almost despaired of. Come to my assistance in this great need that I may receive the consolation and help of heaven in all my necessities, tribulations, and sufferings, particularly *(here make your request)* and that I may praise God with you and all the elect forever I promise, O blessed St Jude, to be ever mindful of this great favor, to always honor you as my special and powerful patron, and to gratefully encourage devotion to you. Amen.

Our Lady of Guadalupe – The Patron Saint of the Americas, she is also known as the *Mother of all Mothers*. She gives hope to the poor and oppressed. Pray to her when you need her most, when you need compassionate yet decisive action.

Our Lady of Guadalupe appeared to Saint Juan Diego on a hillside near Mexico City in the year 1531. Her feast day is celebrated each year on December 12th. He was just an Aztec peasant, and was dazzled by the pure beauty of the Lady. He was told to go to the Bishop and convince him that she was real. Although Juan Diego had no idea how to do this, he did as he was told. She directed he go to the plateau in the dead of winter and gather the flowers there. He did indeed find beautiful flowers which he brought to the Bishop. But when he opened his *tilma,* (a traditional poncho or cloak) not only did an outpouring of Castilian roses pour forth, but also a perfect imprint of the Virgin was imprinted there.

It's the only apparition site where an image has been left. This image hasn't faded in over five hundred years nor has the fabric deteriorated in any way.

Many miracles and cures are credited to Our Lady of Guadalupe. More than ten million people visit her Basilica in Mexico City each year which is the most visited Catholic Church after the Vatican in the world.[11]

There have been attempts made to destroy it. In 1921, someone placed a bomb within flowers at the base of the image of Our Lady of Guadalupe. The marble altar rail was shattered. Windows in houses alongside exploded. A cast iron cross that was next to the image on the cloak was mangled. But not even a crack touched the protective glass that surrounded the *tilma* with the image of Our Lady.

When The Lady asked Juan Diego to build a temple, perhaps she is asking all of us to do the same thing. We can do that by making a shrine in our own hearts. Ask her to intercede for us to God and lay our troubles at her feet.

Novena in Honor of Our Lady of Guadalupe

First Day:
Dearest Lady of Guadalupe, fruitful Mother of holiness, teach me your ways of gentleness and strength. Hear my humble prayer offered with heartfelt confidence to beg this favor.

Second Day:
O Mary, conceived without stain, I come to your throne of grace to share the fervent devotion of your faithful Mexican children who call to you under the glorious Aztec title of Guadalupe. Obtain for me a lively faith to recognize and carry out the divine will always.

Third Day:
O Mary, whose Immaculate Heart was pierced by seven swords of grief, help me to walk valiantly amid the sharp thorns strewn across my pathway. Obtain for me the strength to be a true imitator of you. This I ask you, my dear Mother.

Fourth Day:
Dearest Mother of Guadalupe, I beg you for a fortified will to imitate your divine Son's charity, to always seek the good of others in need.

Fifth Day:
O most holy Mother, I beg you to obtain for me pardon of all my errors, abundant graces to serve the Holy One more faithfully from now on, and lastly, the grace to praise Him with you forever.

Sixth Day:
Mary, Mother of vocations, multiply contemplative inclinations
and fill the earth with sanctuaries and retreats that will be
light and warmth for the world, safety in stormy nights. Beg
the Holy One to send us many spiritual guides.

Seventh Day:
O Lady of Guadalupe, we beg you that parents live a holy life
and educate their children in a sacred manner; that children
honor and follow the directions of their parents; that all
members of the family pray and worship together.

Eighth Day:
With my heart full of the most sincere veneration, I prostrate
myself before you, O Mother, to ask you to obtain for me the
grace to fulfill the duties of my state in life with faithfulness
and constancy.

Ninth Day:
O God, You have been pleased to bestow upon us unceasing
favors by having placed us under the special protection of the
Most Blessed Virgin Mary. Grant us, your humble servants,
who rejoice in honoring her today upon earth, the happiness
of seeing her face to face in heaven.

Hail Mary, full of grace. The Lord is with thee. Blessed art
thou amongst women, and blessed is the fruit of thy womb,
Jesus. Holy Mary, Mother of God, pray for us sinners, now and
at the hour of our death. Amen.[23]

---

23   *Our Lady of Guadalupe,* Edited by Mirabai Starr, 2008
     Mirabai Starr, Sounds True Inc., Boulder, CO.

Saint Philomena - Another saint of impossible or hopeless cases is St Philomena. She is known to be especially powerful in cases involving conversion of sinners, return to the Sacraments, expectant or destitute mothers, unhappiness in the home, children's problems, sterility, money problems, real estate, food for the poor, missions, priest work and mental illness.

Novena Prayer to St Philomena

O Faithful Virgin and glorious martyr, St. Philomena, who works so many miracles on behalf of the poor and sorrowing, have pity on me. Thou knowest the multitude and diversity of my needs. Behold me at thy feet, full of misery, but full of hope. I entreat thy charity, O great Saint! Graciously hear me and obtain from God a favorable answer to the request which I now humbly lay before the...(Here specify your petition.) I am firmly convinced that through thy merits, through the scorn, the sufferings and the death thou didst endure, united to the merits of the Passion and death of Jesus, thy Spouse, I shall obtain what I ask of thee, and in the joy of my heart I will bless God, who is admirable in His Saints, Amen.[24]

Saint Sebastian – Patron Saint of Athletes

For a more complete list of saints as they are associated with other life situations, go to the following website: http://www.americancatholic.org/Features/saints/patrons.asp

---

24   Novena Prayer to St Philomena.

Chapter Suggestions:

- Visualization is a powerful tool. Practice it in your daily life with things as mundane as seeing yourself getting up front parking spaces at the mall. More importantly, visualize yourself getting your hearts desire. Picture it in minute detail including how good you feel as you accomplish or receive whatever it may be. Then give thanks – always give thanks!

- Use an Angel Conversation journal when recording your sessions with your angels. It is easier to have everything all in one place then to have scattered papers everywhere. After the first few sessions, it will get easier and seem more natural. Just open your mind and your heart. You are ready for this or you wouldn't have been drawn to this book. Everything comes to pass for a reason.

- Remember that everyone is not on the same path. You will meet many naysayers and negative people. It's ok. As long as you don't allow them to bring you down, you will be fine. Don't allow yourself to listen to the doom and gloom. Sometimes it will be hard. Ask your angels to help you.

- Keep angels around your home. They are beautiful and they will remind you to listen...

Chapter 4.

Coping with Life's Problems

Life is a series of challenges. How well you face them is how well you live your life.[25]

Prayer is an energy that I believe acts as a catalyst in our lives to increase our productivity, enhance our personal fulfillment, and assist us in acquiring the life lessons we're put on this planet to learn.[26]

Someone recently told me, everyone in life is either right in the middle of adversity, just coming out of adversity or getting ready to go into adversity. When I sat and thought about it, I realized, he was right! Think about your own life for a minute. You have the highs and the lows, but you're always in one of those three cycles. How you react and cope is what is most important.

Try extending yourself in a moment when things in your life aren't great for you and see how quickly your life starts to improve.[27]

---

25 Cindy McCain, Chairman, Hensley & Company. *We Empower,* Maria Shriver 2008 California Governor and First Lady's Conference on Women, New York, NY.
26 *Practical Praying,* John Edward, 2005 by John Edward Princess Books, NY.
27 *Secrets of the Monarch, Allison O. DuBois,* 2007 by Allison DuBois, Published by Fireside Books, a divison of Simon & Schuster Inc.

This reminds me of a favorite story. It has been well publicized although the author is unknown, you may have heard it before. But it fits well with the discussion of coping with life's problems.

> A young man was at the end of his rope. Seeing no way out, he knelt in prayer.
> "Lord, I can't go on," he said. "I have too heavy a cross to bear." The Lord replied,
> "My son, if you cannot bear this weight, just place your cross inside this room,
> Then, open that other door and pick out any cross you wish."
> The man was filled with relief. "Thank you Lord," he sighed, and he did as he was told.
> Upon opening the other door he saw many crosses, some so large the tops were not visible.
> Then he spotted a tiny cross leaning against a far wall. "I'd like that one Lord," he whispered.
> And the Lord replied, "My son, that is the cross you just brought in."[28]

It's true that we all have our crosses to bear. Some are visible for all the world to see, while others are known only to those that carry them.

While it is also true that you can always find someone who is worse off than you are, that doesn't mean that you should trivialize your problems. You need to put things into perspective. Don't go too far into either direction. You don't

---

28 *Prayer,* Author Unknown.

want to end up with the *musobarca* as my Italian mother would say. Translated she always said that meant walking around with a long face or a pout. The actual translation is the face of a cow. Gee thanks, mom!

On the flip side you don't want to be a Pollyanna either. When you do that you are refusing to face reality by constantly only looking at the bright side. We all know people in our lives who fit both extremes.

The *musobarca's* know how to dim the lights in every room. They can't see the good in anything. There is never a silver lining in any cloud. Every conversation always comes back to their problem, and they don't really want to hear any solution. They seem to just want to wallow in it. Woe is me.

The Pollyanna can irritate the heck out of you. Nothing is ever bad enough to warrant feeling down in the dumps. They always want you to look at the bright side. You just broke your leg an hour ago? Look on the bright side! You could have broken both legs! You are forced to feed your family grilled cheese for the second night in a row. Look at the bright side! There are starving people in Ethiopia! Although what she says is true and you know she means well, there is nothing wrong with letting your feelings out and allowing ourselves to feel bad when we feel that way. Remember, feeling down is not a character flaw!

We aren't responsible for all the bad things that are going on around the world. Just because there is someone worse off than us should not in any way make us feel guilty that we are better off or trivialize our problems. Admit that no matter what other tragedies exist in the world, at this moment, your feelings of pain are yours.

> *Even if we don't have cancer, and don't have to suffer through surgery and treatment, we have our own personal difficulties and hardships. I believe God gives us only a heavy a load as we're able to handle. The result is that we're stronger. We're the ones who can encourage and strengthen others in their hardships. I realize now that I shouldn't question God about why certain things happen, especially to good people. I know that good and bad comes into every life. What we need to remember is that God will give us the strength to get through every ordeal.*[29]

We are allowed to feel bad about our troubles. You do not owe an apology to anyone for grieving or feeling bad over the loss of anyone or anything. If others understand, that's nice. It they don't, that's too bad.

---

29   *Daily Devotions Inspired by 90 Minutes in Heaven,* Don Piper and Cecil Murphey, 2006. Berkley Publishing Group, NY. Published by The Penguin Group, New York, NY.

Nothing that grieves us can be called little: by the eternal laws of proportion a child's loss of a doll and a king's loss of a crown are events of the same size.[30]

It is only if we continue to wallow in our problems and not seek to improve our circumstance or let ourselves become a *musobarca* that it becomes a concern.

Feelings are not wrong. Feelings are what they are, and we are allowed to feel them. In fact it isn't healthy to hold them in. Don't ever let anyone tell you differently. You need time to process what you are feeling and to get through the circumstance you are in. You need to do it in a healthy way, and this is where your angels come in. They can help you to cope with the problems you encounter along life's path.

"It's not what happens to us that matters, it's what we do with what happens to us."[31]

Jesus said to his apostles: Do not let your hearts be troubled. Have faith in God, and faith in me.[32]

---

30   *Quote,* Mark Twain.
31   *Heaven is Real,* Don Piper and Cecil Murphey, 2007. Berkley Publishing Group, NY.
32   *The Holy Bible,* John 14:1.

He who has a WHY to live for can bear almost any HOW. [33]

If we always tell ourselves that we can't do something, well we can't. That's why staying positive is so important.

All life is vibration. You combine with what you notice, or you combine with what you vibrate to. If you are vibrating to injustice and resentment you will meet it on your pathway, at every step. [34]

"If anything is big enough to bother you, it's big enough to pray about. The heavenly hand reaches down to us long before we reach up." [35]

Don't worry about anything. Instead, pray about everything. [36]

If we worry, we have no peace. If we worry, we're filled with doubt. If we worry, we don't trust. Ask God to help. [37]

---

33 *Quote,* Nietzsche.
34 *The Power of the Spoken Word,* 2007 by Florence Scovel Shinn, Wilder Publications, Radford, VI.
35 *Heaven is Real,* Don Piper and Cecil Murphey, 2007. Berkley Publishing Group, NY.
36 *The Holy Bible,* Phillipians 4:6.
37 *Daily Devotions Inspired by 90 Minutes in Heaven,* Don Piper and Cecil Murphey, 2006. Berkley Publishing Group, NY. Published by The Penguin Group, New York, NY.

Tell God what you need, and thank him for all he has done.[38]

This will bring you peace!

Moving on after tragedy is not easy. We need some help. We need someone stronger to lean on while we slowly get up and start to walk again. We read stories in the Bible of godly people who endured pain, rejection, heartache and loss but they kept on. They could do that because God was with them, and they had the assurance of the divine presence. God is with you too. He is with all of us, and with him at your side you too can overcome anything.[39]

Nurture your hopes by reading or listening to those who inspire you. Try in turn to inspire those around you.[40]

You have to direct your energy to corners of your life that are deserving of your time and energy and cut your

---

38 *The Holy Bible,* Phillipians 4:6.
39 *Daily Devotions Inspired by 90 Minutes in Heaven,* Don Piper and Cecil Murphey, 2006. Berkley Publishing Group, NY. Published by The Penguin Group, New York, NY.
40 Mariane Pearl, Author, Wife of Journalist Daniel Pearl, *We Empower,* Maria Shriver 2008 California Governor and First Lady's Conference on Women, New York, NY.

losses in areas that don't pay off emotionally, spiritually and even financially. When you help someone do something that is emotionally fulfilling to you, it strengthens your soul. You can actually feel a great satisfaction from within. When that happens you know you've done something that sends out positive energy.

I'd like to share a personal story with you. I've taken these excerpts from my journal from my first retreat.

March 4, 2004
Loyola of the Lakes
Day One

I remember every year that my dad made his retreat at Loyola of the Lakes. Sometimes I would accompany my brother to drop dad off. I think he did it every year for over 20 years or more.

Back then they were silent retreats, even during dinner. After dad died, followed in three months by mom, I told myself I would like to make a retreat at Loyola of the Lakes. Four years have passed, but finally here I am.

Upon looking over the schedule for the weekend, I am happy to see that there is little structure. I am here this weekend for alone time. I need quiet reflection and time for meditation. I feel very close to mom and dad here in this place.

… I just returned from the first presentation of the

weekend. I found myself growing sleepy and sneaking glances at my watch. But then something changed. The moderator said to forget about your problems and empty your mind.

I was a little surprised at this because I thought I would spend the time concentrating on my problems and a way to solve them. But he said Let Go and Let God. I'd never heard these words before. They stilled me, and they reached me to my core.

Think about these words as it pertains to your life. Allow yourself to Let Go and Let God. Relinquish control of your life. Pray to God and your angels to help you. Stop trying to work out the details of how things will work themselves out. Just pray about it. Let it go and leave the rest up to Him.

... He also talked about our spiritual batteries and our spiritual light. It may go dim, but it never goes out. Everything we do from doing laundry, to bringing food to the sick to babysitting is food for our light. I never looked at it that way.

He reminded us of the picture of Jesus knocking on the door. I always thought of that picture in terms of sickness, like It's your time, and Jesus is coming for you. But I never realized that the door has no doorknob, and Jesus was knocking so we could let him in. The door represents our heart, and it only opens from the inside to let Jesus inside. I was overcome at that moment to tears. I will never look at that picture the same way again. It was very powerful.

After the Blessed Sacrament was displayed, we knelt and said a short prayer. I pictured myself wrapping in three separate boxes my problems. I pictured tying a string tightly around them and giving them to God to place on a shelf for the weekend. I hope to clear my mind and open my heart to hear the Lord talk to me, to hear my parents visit me in my dreams. To help me.

Take a moment to picture the things that are troubling you. Imagine wrapping them inside a box and tying it with a string. Picture yourself placing them on a shelf. Now open your heart and trust God to take the control away from you. Stop the constant worrying about these issues. Trust him. Ask your angels to help you.

Day Two

...Two things have stuck with me. One is to light lots of candles, or at least always keep one burning in plain sight. The light of the candle represents God. The flicker of the light is God's presence. I envision looking at the light and feeling peace.

The second thing is the question that the moderator asked: "How many things can a person do in a lifetime?" The answer that popped into my head was *Infinity*. But he wanted a number, so I said "Millions". Well the answer was Two. We can choose to do the right or good thing or we can choose the wrong or bad thing. Only Two.

...We had a discussion of the wolf within us. On one side our hearts are hard with fear, anger arrogance, envy, self-pity, greed, lies and jealousy. On the other side our hearts are soft with joy, peace, serenity, kindness, compassion, empathy and friendship. Both wolves can live within you, but the one you feed is the one that wins!

Think about it. Decide which wolf you want to feed.

Day Three

...The question was asked what touched us this weekend. After a brief moment of panic, I gathered my thoughts and raised my hand. I started by saying that this was my first retreat I'd ever attended. This statement was met with applause, much to my surprise! I continued by telling how my dad always came on retreat to Loyola and how it took me four years to act on my intention to come. I said that I didn't know what to expect but did think I would spend the time this weekend working on my problems. So when we were told to *Let Go and Let God,* I was surprised. But I did that, and it worked. And I thank you for that.

...Those words *Let Go and Let God* had a profound effect on me. I had a need to relinquish most of the control I feel rules my daily life and just *Let God.* Those packages that I had God place on the shelf for me – I decided this morning to leave them tightly wrapped and on the shelf for God to handle. I'll leave those key issues that have been weighing so heavily on my mind. I'll leave them and *Let Go* and thereby *Let God.*

Thank you Lord for filling my heart this weekend. Help me to keep your light alive in my life.

Can you just let go? Can you let go of the control that rules your daily life so you can Let God?

Be certain not to squander your life. Take the time to inspire others through your strength and affection. Make sure the story of your life is something that you're proud of. If it's not, then you have work to do. Anyone can sit back and watch life pass them by, but it takes heart to jump in the game and play.[41]

You don't get to choose how you're going to die. Or when. You can only decide how you're going to live. Now.[42]

I think the perfect ending to this chapter is with another of my favorite stories. It is another popular one that you have most likely heard. But it captures perfectly man's struggle with life's trials and tribulations and God's never-ending love for us.

Footprints in the Sand
By Mary Stevenson

One night a man had a dream. He dreamed he was walking along the beach with the LORD. Across the sky flashed scenes from his life. For each scene, he noticed two sets of footprints

---

41 *Secrets of the Monarch, Allison O. DuBois,* 2007 by Allison DuBois, Published by Fireside Books, a divison of Simon & Schuster Inc.
42 *Quote,* Joan Baez.

in the sand: one belonging to him, and the other to the LORD.

When the last scene of his life flashed before him he looked back, at the footprints in the sand. He noticed that many times along the path of his life there was only one set of footprints. He also noticed that it happened at the very lowest and saddest times of his life.

This really bothered him and he questioned the LORD about it: "LORD, you said that once I decided to follow you, you'd walk with me all the way. But I have noticed that during the most troublesome times in my life there is only one set of footprints. I don't understand why when I needed you most you would leave me."

The LORD replied: "My son, My precious child, I love you and I would never leave you, During your times of trial and suffering, when you see only one set of footprints, it was then that I carried you."[43]

Chapter Suggestions:

- The analogy of candles to God is an especially visual one. Remembering that the light of the candle represents God and the flicker of the light signifies his presence is very peaceful. Candles can be found in many colors and varieties to match every décor. You can even buy votive candles with flameless lights if you have little ones around.

---

43   *Footprints in the Sand,* Mary Stevenson.

- Do your spiritual batteries need charged? Just like we need food for our bodies, we also need food for our souls. If everything we do is food for our light, make sure we take care of ourselves by nourishing our souls. Take care what you expose yourselves to in the relationships you have, the entertainment you watch, the books you read. Don't put anything toxic in.

- Get a picture of Jesus knocking on the door to remind yourself to let him into your heart. Display it in your home where you can look at it often.

- Display a small, brightly wrapped gift somewhere on a shelf in your home. The significance is that your troubles are being kept for God to control, not you. Let Go and Let God.

- Try to take the opportunity to attend a weekend retreat once a year if possible. It is good for the soul.

Chapter 5:

Importance of Gratitude

Number 1 on your To Do List every day: Gratitude. This brings grace, ease, pleasure and productivity to your day.[44]

Are you a grateful person? Do you send handwritten thank you notes when you receive a gift? Or when someone has done something especially thoughtful for you? Have you taught your children to do so? A personal expression of gratitude is so important and should not be lost in this fast-paced electronic world we live in of emails and phone calls. Believe me I love my cell phone and laptop computer. But they will not and should not replace the handwritten thank you note or personal note. Ever. These tell the recipient that you care enough to take the time to thank them for the gift they took the time to select, the money they cared enough to send, the time they spent with you, or whatever it was they did for you. Don't let this become a lost art!

No duty is more urgent than that of returning thanks.[45]

---

44 *Simple Abundance: A Daybook of Comfort and Joy,* Sarah Ban Breathnuch. 1995 by Sarah Ban Breathnuch. Warner Books Inc, NY.

45 *Quote,* Saint Ambrose.

There is always enough for the needy but never enough for the greedy.[46]

We must show gratitude for the blessings we receive in our life as well. Take a minute right now and make a list of everything that you are grateful for in your life. The list can be as long as you like.

Here is an example of a gratitude list:

my family

my health

healthy children & grandchildren

warm bed at night

food on the table

possessions

nice neighbors

good neighborhood

freedom

choices

God's patience

eyesight

snuggling up with a good book

good memory

a husband who puts up with me

ability to juggle many balls at once (figuratively speaking)

my dog

loving relatives

good friends

ability to get up each morning

---

46   *The Power of Giving,* Azim Jamal & Harvey McKinnon, 2005, 2008, the Penguin Group, New York, NY.

inspiration for ideas   having work I love to do
God's love   freshly washed sheets

Have you ever looked at your checkbook balance and found it was short by – oh let's say $293 of the mortgage payment or car payment or any important bill? Then as if by magic, what do you do if you receive almost that exact amount by a totally unexpected means? I suppose you dance a little jig!

This has happened to me many times. Sometimes I've received several small checks that make up the total missing amount. The source is always unexpected and I always make sure I say a prayer of sincere gratitude and thanksgiving for the gift in my time of need.

I can't stress how important gratitude must become part of your daily life. Appreciating what you have in your life will help you feel less anxious about what you don't have. When you are genuinely grateful you are not greedy and are more likely to attract to you more of what you want.

There is a excerpt from a song that says, *It's not having what you want, it's wanting what you've got. (Soak Up the Sun* by Sheryl Crow[47]) Those words are very true. Take it one step further, and be grateful for what you have.

St Francis of Assisi said *"For It Is In Giving That We*

---

47   Music *"Soak Up the Sun"*, By Sheryl Crow, Warner/ Chappell Music Inc., Warner-Tamerlane Publishing Corp, Old Crow Music.

Receive". For the longest time I didn't really understand what that meant.

Real abundance comes to us when we share what we have, even when we don't have anything to share. When you reach into your wallet and pull that last $1 bill out and give it to that bell ringer freezing for the Salvation Army collection bucket, that's sharing.

When you take that last $5 bill out of your wallet you were going to treat yourself to a Coffee Mocha at Starbucks you haven't had in months and give it instead for the collection in church for the missions, that's sharing.

When you reach into your food pantry that's pretty low because it's four more days until payday, and you pull out the last two boxes of Kraft macaroni and cheese for the church food cupboard even though that means it's just tomato soup and peanut butter for you, that's sharing.

When you donate your kid's used clothes to a charity that benefits children instead of taking them to the local consignment shop, that's sharing. Or, when you donate your gently used household items and small appliances to your local domestic violence project, that's sharing.

And when you donate money in any denomination to the charity of your choice, that too is sharing. For when we give, only then can we receive, and the circle just continues. And our gratitude continues and grows as does our abundance.

Remember,

A wise man I know said many times, *"It is possible to sell without serving, but it is impossible to serve without selling."* Apply that to all areas of your life.

Finding happiness all comes back to giving. If you want to find happiness, you need to give it. If you want wealth, you need to give wealth. If you want love, you need to give love.[48] For in the words of St Francis, it is only in giving that you receive.

Giving enriches your life with meaning, fulfillment and happiness. Always give of your time, talent and treasure and you too can experience the beauty of those gifts in return.

It is good to give when things are going great in your life, but you can also give in times of hardship. When giving during these times of hardship, you may tend to forget your problems and find solutions to your challenges. The amount you give is up to you. The more you give, the more you receive. The reward may be immediate, or it may take awhile., but no giving goes unnoticed by the universal laws of nature.[49]

Each day should begin and end with a grateful heart, thanking God for his many blessings in our lives. Be grateful for now, <u>this minute</u>, for it is all you have. Don't waste your now's living in the past and worrying about the future. Your true happiness exists only in the present.

---

48   *The Power of Giving,* Azim Jamal & Harvey McKinnon, 2005, 2008, the Penguin Group, New York, NY.
49   *The Power of Giving,* Azim Jamal & Harvey McKinnon, 2005, 2008, the Penguin Group, New York, NY.

The present moment is filled with joy and happiness. If you are attentive, you will see it.[50]

Let go of the past. If you carry it around like luggage, you won't be able to move forward.[51]

The "Bad"...

Do not seek to have events happen as you want them to, but instead want them to happen as they do happen, and your life will go well.[52]

We can plan. We can hope. But we can't determine what will happen. When those powerful events come and change our lives, some psychologists refer to them as markers. A marker can be something as simple as a girl wearing makeup for the first time or a teen getting a drivers license. Their lives are changed afterward. Sometimes not dramatically, but life becomes different. We have markers all throughout life. As soon as we realize we have a new marker, we have to reconfigure our lives. We may have known what we wanted to do if life continued as it was, but the rules have all changed. The markers force us to make a new game plan. It's not easy to shift our way of thinking or move away from our old behavior, but that's what life's markers require us to

---

50   *Quote,* Thich Nhat Hanh.
51   Chiqui Cartagena, Hispanic Expert & Managing Director of Integrated Marketing at Meredith Hispanic Ventures. *We Empower,* Maria Shriver 2008 California Governor and First Lady's Conference on Women, New York, NY.
52   *Quote,* Epictetus.

do. During all of this we should pause and ask, what is it that God wants me to do?[53]

But what about the things that happen in our lives that we perceive as bad? Let me tell you a story…

It was the summer of 2007. The day began early as I prepared for a summer picnic with the entire family. I went to the basement to retrieve the paper products that were stored in a plastic container. The basement at that time was finished with carpeting and paneling. As soon as I stepped onto the carpeting, I knew something was wrong. The carpet was completely saturated with water, making squelching sounds with each step I took.

I could see the boxes that were directly onto the floor were soaking wet. I immediately called for my husband, Skip, to come downstairs to help me find the source of the water leak. He quickly found that our water holding tank had sprung a leak. Since it was Sunday, there was little we could do except to turn off the water until the next day when a replacement tank could be obtained.

Meanwhile we surveyed the damage. We were looking at a room approximately 40 feet long and 14 feet wide with water damage. Unfortunately for us, this room was full of stuff!

Since we had the family picnic that day that we happened

53   *Daily Devotions Inspired by 90 Minutes in Heaven,* Don Piper and Cecil Murphey, 2006. Berkley Publishing Group, NY. Published by The Penguin Group, New York, NY.

to be hosting, we didn't have time to further examine the extent of the damage. So we grabbed the plastic container that held our paper products that we needed for the day, hooked up the dehumidifier and headed out to enjoy our family. My husband gave me good advice which was to put this mess out of my mind, but I found it difficult to heed his words.

My first instinct was to have our two adult sons rip out the wet carpeting, but somehow that never happened. *Angelwhisper #1.*

The first thing we did the next morning was call a plumber who came and installed a new water holding tank. Less than a week later, I went to the basement to find water pouring in, pretty much in the same location. It was soon discovered that we had a leak in the outside piping that led to our well. This had been there awhile and had been causing a slow leak that had been draining behind the paneling and under the carpet for a long time unbeknownst to us. At this point I called the insurance company. The adjuster suggested we get several heavy duty blowers in to blow the air around and generally dry things out.

For some reason, I held off on getting those blowers. *Angelwhisper #2*

I had a mold test done and found we had several types of mold, some toxic. The worst thing was that we had black mold. Known as Stachybotrys mold, it is the variety of mold that will induce fear and most definitely get the attention of your insurance company. It is somewhat rare where I live, and it is deadly.

You see, the very worst thing that you can do when you have black mold is to make it airborne. Ripping out the carpet and getting those heavy duty blowers would have been the absolute worst thing I could have done when dealing with black mold. That could have released the spores into the air and contaminated my whole house.

As it was, all of the spores were contained within the carpet and within the walls of the paneling. The removal had to be done precisely and in an enclosed environment. This should never be done by amateurs or by someone not wearing protective gear. My entire basement, along with the entryways, were sealed off. The remediation experts wore what looked like space suits, and my basement was de-contaminated. Plus we filled a fifteen-yard dumpster with all the stuff we lost.

During this time my husband was out of work and struggling with a medical crisis. Funny, but we had a "flood" at work at the same time. It seemed everywhere I turned I was surrounded by an abundance of water. I felt overwhelmed. I am a firm believer that everything happens for a reason, everything has a purpose for good. But I remember asking God, "Is this a test? Help me cope with this! Please!" While what I later called "Flood #1" seemed like a bad thing, really ended up to be a good thing. While it was happening, I couldn't imagine ever thinking I would think it was good. My goodness, so much all at once. My husband's medical crisis, financial worries and now a double water woe. But with the water issues came an insurance check that helped with the financial worries. And later we found that we were sitting on a time bomb with that black mold. So the flood was a blessing enabling us to take care of that festering problem that could have wreaked havoc on our health and caused us to lose our home. We had much to be grateful for!

If you notice, I said "Flood #1", so that must mean there was a "Flood #2". Indeed. Six months after the work was complete, there was a power outage that lasted twelve hours. Enough time for the dual sump pumps to back up six inches of water across the entire basement, not just the half that had been refinished, but the entire basement. This time I knew enough to immediately pull up carpet as I knew mold can start within forty-eight hours and I wasn't going to go through that again!

This time I really organized. We filled another fifteen-yard dumpster. We built shelves. The one side was completely empty. But as I said, things happen for a reason. There is a purpose for good.

Two months later, my sister-in-law – my husband's sister, Natalie, died suddenly from a pulmonary embolism. Their mother had lived with her. So in the blink of an eye, all of our lives changed. Their house had to be sold and mountains of belongings had to be sorted. Had we not had our "floods", we wouldn't have had the room to enable mom's things to move into our now empty basement so she didn't have to part with so many possessions at a time when decisions were difficult to make. We painted our guest room upstairs and we welcomed mom into our home.

I know it has been very hard for mom. She is 83 years old, and she lost her daughter, Natalie so suddenly. She was uprooted from the home she knew for the past six years. Natalie's house was sold to settle the estate. But this only happened after four months of work to clear the house.

Mom was a child of the depression, and it is very difficult for her to get rid of anything. So she wanted to go through every single item herself. It was a slow process. I knew we had a clear basement and told her she could bring along anything she wanted. We filled several skids with boxes for her to go through at her leisure.

Now that mom is settled in with us and the house is sold, things are evening out. Mom is still grieving as we all are. But I believe there are lessons in everything. For her, perhaps it is a time to spend with her son, enjoy more of a closeness that she has longed for I think for many years. For my husband, it is a time to spend with his mother, make a peace with times from the past.

For me, I have opened my heart to someone hurting and in need and am learning patience and tolerance as I hope my children will continue to show me when I enter into my old age. For both mom and me, we have moved into a closer relationship that I feel will get even closer with each passing day.

While I miss Natalie, I am grateful for the chance to love her mother in a way I wouldn't have had the opportunity if not like this. I came across the following lines the other day in my reading: *"There's something that God wants you to do that you never would have been able to do if this had not happened"*.[54] I pray everyday to be worthy of this service.

Postscript: Shortly before this book went to press, my husband's other sister, Marilyn died. Mom has lost two daughters in just five short months.

Some things happen to us from which we never recover, and they disrupt the normalcy of our lives. That's how life is. Human nature has a tendency to try to reconstruct old ways and pick up where we left off. We must instead forget the old standard and accept a New Normal. ...it doesn't change the way things are. The sooner I make peace with that fact and accept the way things are, the sooner I'll be able to live in peace and enjoy my new normalcy.[55]

Be grateful even when it is very hard. Don't get caught up in the little things that don't matter. The little things are

---

54   *Here If You Need Me,* Kate Braestrup 2007 by Kate Braestrup, Little Brown and Company NY.

55   *The Circle: How the Power of a Single Wish Can Change Your Life, Laura Day,* 2001 by Laura Day. Published by the Penguin Group, New York, NY.

what can trip you up, I know because they get to me too! Just pray to God for strength and guidance. Your angels will help you. Focus on the positive. Thank God each morning for all the blessings that you have. Ask for help in coping with your problems and adversities. You do attract into your life what you put out there. If you put out into the world anger and hostility, that's what you will get back. Plus it doesn't make the journey very pleasant either. Instead, take the higher path with God's grace try to accept each new adversity with gratitude.

I'm human too. I haven't accepted all the bumps in my life graciously, I'll admit that. And I know that patience and tolerance are virtues I constantly need to work on. But the closer you stay to God, the easier it gets. It's an easier walk with him than without, I can tell you that.

Let Go and Let God. There is meaning in that phrase. I have always been the type of person who loves to control things. I love to control the order of my household. I love to control the menu on holidays. I love to control our spending, our social calendar, our vacation destinations, etc. I guess you could say I'm a control freak. There, I've said it. All it

83

takes is one uncontrollable medical crisis or other unplanned household event and suddenly you are no longer In Control.

You might fight for the wheel for a little while. But the sooner you realize that you can't drive, the better off you'll be. That's when you just Let Go and Let God do what he's planned for you. Just go along and see what happens. You just may be surprised at what is around the corner when you do that.

> *Learn to get in touch with the silence within yourself and know that everything in this life has a purpose.*[56]

> *In the middle of difficulty lies opportunity.*[57]

We don't know what lies ahead. Only God knows that.

> *Often God shuts a door in our face, And then subsequently opens the door through which we need to go.*[58]

---

56 *Quote*, Elisabeth Kubler-Ross.
57 *Quote*, Albert Einstein.
58 *Quote*, Catherine Marshall.

Often times the things we think we really want, the things we think are best for us may not be. For instance:

That relationship.
That job.
That bid for the new house.

Then after we haven't gotten our heart's desires we realize it was best that we didn't get them after all. But at the time we were hurt! And angry! At everybody – and at God!

That relationship we wanted to work out so badly. He left for someone else and you were heartbroken. You railed at God because you wanted it so badly. You tried so hard! You poured your heart and soul into that union! Why did God not want you to be happy? But two years later you met your soul mate and now you have a relationship that is so good, so wonderful. You are happier than you could ever have dreamed possible. How grateful you are for this love of your life that God sent you!

That job that you tried so desperately to get. You were willing to sacrifice precious time with your family for that promotion because the money was so good. But you didn't get the job. Didn't God see how hard you worked? You were so disgusted. You snapped at your family for two weeks and didn't go to church for two months. Then six months later your company merged and you were promoted at a better salary than you would have had without having to sacrifice time with your family. How grateful you are to God for this opportunity to support your family without having to sacrifice time with them!

The new house bid fell through as another couple topped your bid. You were disconsolate for weeks. But then a month later a new listing appeared for a larger house in a better school district. This time your bid won out. Then, you found out there was structure problems on the other house. How grateful you are to God to have the good fortune to be able to move your family into this comfortable home and avoid the problem issues on the other dwelling!

These examples are real. The relationship was my niece. The job was my friend. And the house bid was my daughter. Sometimes what God has in store for us is better than anything we can think up on our own. Dream Big. With God all things are possible.

Many people pray and receive the answer to their

prayers, but ignore them or deny them, because the answers didn't come in the expected form.[59]

Another thing that is important to remember is that we usually don't realize the effect our life has on others, be it good or bad. This point is made well in the much-loved classic movie *"It's A Wonderful Life"*. There have been two versions made. While they are both good, I prefer the original with Jimmy Stewart as George Bailey. The film takes you to a point where George thinks he wouldn't have been missed had he never been born. His angel "Clarence" shows him what the world would have been like if that would have been the case. It was quite an eye opener for George. He comes away from the experience with a new appreciation for his family, for life and a new zest for living.

The people who seem the most troubled are those who can't accept the changes in their lives.[60]

---

59   *The Goddess in Every Girl,* M. J. Abadie, 2002 by M. J. Abadie Bindu Books, Rochester, Vermont.

60   *Daily Devotions Inspired by 90 Minutes in Heaven,* Don Piper and Cecil Murphey, 2006. Berkley Publishing Group, NY. Published by The Penguin Group, New York, NY.

John Edward sums it up in his book *Practical Praying:*

I learned that while you may not receive exactly what you think you're praying for, your prayers will likely bring you what you need... as well as what God intends for you as part of the "bigger plan."[61]

If you haven't read any of John's books, I urge you to do so. They include: *After Life: Answers from the Other Side, Crossing Over, Final Beginnings, One Last Time: A Psychic Medium Speaks to Those We've Loved and Lost, What if God were the Sun?* and *Practical Praying.* High on my list of recommendations!

Health

A study at the University of Chicago in 2003 suggests that a lifetime of fearful stress takes an accumulated toll on our health. Fearful people tend not to live as long.[62]

Jesus said *"So don't worry about tomorrow. Tomorrow will bring its own worries"*[63]

If you've ever had surgery, you'd like to skip over the recovery and just feel good again. It doesn't work that

---

61   *Practical Praying,* John Edward, 2005 by John Edward
      Princess Books, NY.
62   *Changing Your Course the 5 Step Guide to Getting the
      Life You Want,* Bob & Melinda Blanchard. 2008, Sterling
      Publishing Co Inc. New York, NY.
63   *The Holy Bible,* Matthew 6:34.

way. We have to earn the right to feel good again by going through the ordeal of persevering through the hurting times and enduring the pain. Patience is absolutely critical. If we don't develop the ability to hold on and keep fighting, we just don't make it. Enduring the ordeal of therapy and recovery often means persevering through hard, hurting times. There's a famous illustration about a person who saw the caterpillar about to change into a butterfly. The creature struggled to get out of the chrysalis. The would-be-helpful-person removed the butterfly to stop the painful ordeal. He got the butterfly out, but it could never fly. The struggle makes butterflies able to fly. Enduring the slow, painful hardship allows endurance to develop. We may not like the ordeals we face, but if we're going to soar or even survive, we have to go through those times. We also have to do it at the right time. Not too early, and not too late. And most of all, we have to be kind to ourselves and not get frustrated over our lack of patience. Those who are committed to living the easy way miss this important ingredient of a good life. The struggles make us stronger.[64]

We all tend to see our lives only from our own tiny vantage point. It is human nature to look at our own problems and try to figure them out. The following poem, called "Life's Weaving", whose author is unknown, talks about each of our lives being just a part of the grand design of God's plan. I especially love it, and I think it's a perfect way to end this chapter.

---

64 *Daily Devotions Inspired by 90 Minutes in Heaven,* Don Piper and Cecil Murphey, 2006. Berkley Publishing Group, NY. Published by The Penguin Group, New York, NY.

Life's Weaving

Life is but a weaving
between my God and me;
I may not choose the colors,
He knows what they should be.

For He can view the pattern
Upon the upper side,
While I can see it only
On this, the under side.

Sometimes He weaveth sorrow,
Which seemeth strange to me;
But I will trust His judgment,
And work on faithfully.

'Tis He who fills the shuttle,
He knows just what is best;
So I shall weave in earnest
And leave with Him the rest.

At last, when life is ended,
With Him I shall abide,
And I may view the pattern
Upon the upper side,

Then I shall know the reason
Why pain with joy entwined,
Was woven in the fabric
Of life that God designed.[65]

---

65   *Prayer,* Author Unknown.

Chapter Suggestions:

- Start to notice the books that come across your path. They are messages that you need to hear. Be especially aware if a particular title crosses your path more than once. If that happens, by all means, get the book! You might read about a book somewhere and it interests you, then it may be suggested by a friend and you might hear it being suggested on TV or on the radio. These are all nudges to you.

  This happened to me recently with the book "The Shack" by William P. Young. It was recommended to me by a friend because she knew I was going through some personal things that I would benefit from the story. Then I came across a write up about the book. So I got on the list at two libraries to read it, but I was 22nd on one list and 36th on the other. Two weeks later, the book was given to me as a gift by another friend. I believe I was supposed to read that book!

  Hint: I go to the library a lot, I also belong to a book club and cut out clippings of books that strike my fancy that I want to read. I also cut out clippings from magazines or newspaper articles. I keep these in a little pouch separated by fiction and non-fiction.

  I used to read primarily fiction. Now I read almost

exclusively non-fiction with just a smattering of fiction thrown in when I just want to escape and be entertained by my favorite author. When I go to the library, I choose the books from my pre-selected titles in my little "library pouch". I prefer this method rather than just browsing the aisles which I rarely if ever do.

However, the other day I did exactly that finding myself browsing the recent arrival shelf. I picked up and checked out a book called *Awakened Instincts* by Mary Rose Occhino. Just a couple of lines on the inside jacket cover intrigued me so I decided to check out the book. I read this on the second page of the introduction: ...*"It's no coincidence that you found this book, or that this book has found you. Take this as a sign from the universe, and from those who guide you, that this book didn't just accidentally fall into your hands..."* OK, right then I knew I was going to love this book!

- Start a Gratitude Journal – Write in it every evening to get into the practice of bringing gratitude into your life as a daily practice. You can write just a few lines, whatever sparks to you. It is for your eyes only, so it doesn't have to be profound. What is important is that you get in the habit of being grateful for the blessings in your life.

- Consider mediation. This can be whatever time of day that fits your schedule. You will find it soothing and restful. It clears your mind of the clutter of daily living and brings you close to God.

Chapter 6:

Angelwhispers

Angelic beings are continually ministering to people in many ways in these present days. Many seeming coincidences are really angels on the job![66]

The Bell

Excerpt from my journal/January 2001:

...At my father's funeral mass, my nephew, Rick gave a wonderful eulogy. He delivered a warm message and ended it by playing a tape – one of dad's. As his voice boomed over the microphone, I cried. He said how proud he was of his five childrens. (He always referred to us as childrens not children) The tape ended as all his tapes ended, but this time it had special meaning. He said *"Until we meet again, So Long!"*

That evening we gathered with our mother at the assisted living facility apartment that she had shared with dad. She was frail, suffering from lung cancer, and had told her nurse that she had to be strong for her kids and get through the funeral. Now, mom had done exactly that. She was napping when all of us heard the bathroom door creak and someone said *"Mom's*

---

66   *The Gift of Angels: Inspirational Encounters with God's Heavenly Messengers,* 2003 by Zondervan, Grand Rapids, MI, Compiler: Rebecca Currington in conjunction with Snapdragon Editorial Group Inc.

up". I started to move to get up when there was an awful thump and a yell. I jumped up so fast and ran to mom. I found her on the bathroom floor, still in her black dress and hose. Her head was way up in the corner under the sink. I gently lifted her and saw she wasn't banged up. I held her to me and gently rocked her. She was keening, a low moan, sort of a wail. I held her as she cried. She kept putting both of her hands to both sides of her head, rocking and saying *"Where's Vic? Where's Vic? Where's Vic?"*

Later that night at home with my husband, I was telling him how worried I was about mom. Would she be able to stay in her apartment? Or would she have to move to *"The Other Side"*? That was mom's name for the skilled care section of the facility, the section that she feared. As I was talking I was working on the roses I had taken from the flower spray that had been on my dad's casket. I had three of them that I was going to hang on the wall up by their pictures. I was in the process of tying some ribbons onto them, when my dog, Clipper, started to act weird.

He was standing in front of the bookshelves and kept boosting up and down onto nothing. My husband, Skip, said *"Your dad must be here petting Clipper."* Dad always liked Clipper. He would say *"He's a good little dog."* He would pet him and let him have the last of the food on his plate when he would be over for dinner. I said *"Clipper, where's Grandpa?"* Clipper looked over at the table, then back at me. I said again, *"Clipper, where's Grandpa?"* Again, Clipper looked over at the table, then back at me. Skip said, *"He must be sitting at the table."*

My chair was kind of pulled out, and the angel figurine in a basket that my friend, Ann sent me was right there on the table. So I went over and just started talking. *"Dad, do you like this basket? Ann sent it to me because she knew how important angels were to you. Dad, we need your help. We're so worried about mom. She's just a mess. We don't know if she can stay in your apartment. We're just so worried. She was so pitiful tonight."* As I was saying all of this, I continued to tie the roses.

I pulled a chair over and stood on the chair to hang them. Skip had been sitting watching TV and changing channels. He randomly stopped at one show that was talking about Chinese porcelain. They said you can always tell when it's real porcelain because it has a unique sound to it. It sounds like a bell. Then three distinct bells chimed – DING! DING! DING! I stopped with my arms in mid-air. I looked at the TV in shock and then at Skip. He said *"That was your dad!"* I was filled with joy, and I knew that it indeed was dad, telling me he heard me and my worries for mom. I knew he would watch over her. It was incredible.

You see, I have been telling dad for a year or more that when the time came, ring a bell for me. And I always reminded him of it when we talked spiritual talk. As the time got closer, we talked about it more.

At Thanksgiving everyone was at the table and Dad pulled me over and said *"Next year, I won't be here, but I'll ring the bell!"* He had smiled when he said it, and had tears in his eyes. As the months went by, now and then I would remind him about the bell. Just a few days before he died, when the bell came up again he said to me *"Now honey, God has to tell me it's ok to ring the bell. If he says I can't, then I can't do it. I don't want you to be disappointed."* Dad must have gotten permission!

Nurse's Message

Excerpts from my journal/March 2001

We have the schedule figured out for staying with mom. My sister, Pat, and I will take turns doing the overnights. Then I will schedule nursing help to cover the days when everybody is working. This way I could still work both my full-time and part-time job plus finish my Italian classes (only two more!). In order for mom to stay on the assisted living side, she needs somebody with her all of the time, so this seems to be the best way to handle it. I took the first of the night shifts.

Mom was in bed by 8PM and asleep. At 9PM I was tired. I'd been awake since 4AM, so I lay down next to her. I don't know if my lying down confused her because nobody has slept with her since Dad. She knew who I was but was very agitated. She kept picking at the blankets and tried to get out of bed at least six times. She would reach and grab at something in the air often talking out loud to my dad. She was agitated, confused and incoherent. It was a long night.

I realized during those long hours before 3AM when I finally slept that I couldn't do the nights, and there was no way I thought Pat could or should. I knew that if I didn't get my rest at night, I will get sick. It so happened that two days before

Kathy, one of my favorite nurses, asked me if I was interested in people who could help with care. She said she knew of someone. I wasn't convinced but agreed to take the name. She said she'd get it for me, then I pretty much forgot about it. Last night, Kathy called and gave me the name of an aide and her phone number. I still didn't really think I needed it.

Sometime between 1AM and 3AM it hit me – schedule care for the nights, Pat can do days, and I'll do afternoons. Kathy was meant to deliver that message to me because God knew that last night it would occur to me that I couldn't handle the nights.

So I called the aide, and she is free tonight! She said her mother lives out of town, so she cares for elderly people to give back in the hopes that someone else is doing the same for her mother. Isn't that something? God sent this special person to us.

Another amazing thing: Pat lost her job two days ago. That makes her free to handle the days. God works in mysterious ways...

Not My Time

...As I arrived to relieve my brother, Lee and his wife, Dorothy, they told me that mom had been asking and asking when I was coming – as usual and watching the clock. I was also informed that mom said she was taking me with her! Lee hugged me when they left and said *"Don't go along!"* I said *"No, I wasn't planning on it!"* Mom was sitting up and alert and rather feisty.

She was talking about dad's having been there and kept telling me that I was going and wouldn't it be nice! I kept saying no, I'm not going. I'm not ready. I have work to do on earth still, it's not my time. She told me *"Why don't you want to see your father? I'm disappointed in you. You don't want to go with your father."* And on and on it went. She wouldn't let up.

It was really freaking me out and starting to upset me. I went to the bathroom, and while I was in there I said, *"Dad, please help her to stop telling me I'm going unless I'm supposed to be prepared for something. I hope this isn't my time..."*

When I came out of the bathroom, mom never mentioned it again.

Angel Heartstrings

Excerpts from my journal/April 2001:

...She is hardly aware of my presence. Instead she seems to be turning within. Looking at her face I can't believe she'll make it through the weekend. I know I said this before, but this time something is different. She opens her eyes again. I look at her, and she smiles and says "How do you always know when I open my eyes?"...

...She has been alert the whole time I've been here – watching the Indians game. Her conversation hasn't made any sense. At 11PM when I was going to leave, she didn't want me to go. When I tried to say good night to her she shook her finger at me and said, *"You're not leaving ! No you're not!"* Since she was still wide awake, I sat back down. At 11:45PM though I knew I had to go. I told her I had to get up early. She grumbled a little, but we said our goodbyes. I told her I loved her, she said she loved me too. I gave her a hug and a kiss and squeezed her hand. As I left, I saw that love shining brightly in her eyes as I had always seen there my entire life…As it ended up, that was our last conversation. She went downhill after that, never really awakening enough to converse or know any of us. She died one week later.

Angel Josephine

…Skip worked it out that we could go to Myrtle Beach leaving Monday after the funeral and not coming back until the following Friday. It was exactly what I needed. A bridge between my grief and reality…A neat, wacky thing happened. The TV was on, but nobody was watching. I switched channels again and again and stopped at this funky cartoon. All of a sudden one of the characters of the cartoon was on the screen – and her name was *Angel Josephine!* I was startled. Then I smiled. I believed I was supposed to see that. If I didn't already know it, I should know that mom is now with the angels…

Angelwhisper Message

I was in that hazy place between sleep and wakefulness when I heard from the television that was on in our bedroom a news report about Vice President Dick Cheney. I wasn't paying attention, but something in the report must have seeped through my semi-conscious state. The report was talking about the symptoms of deep vein thrombosis (DVT), aching in the calf, redness, warmth in the area, tenderness or swelling. If you have any of these symptoms, the report cautioned, go to your doctor. Also known as *"The Silent Killer"*, DVT are often ignored because of the slight symptoms they exhibit. Cheney had been diagnosed with DVT after complaining of mild calf paid after returning from a trip to Asia. Undiagnosed, DVT can be fatal. Somehow I heard these words and snapped awake.

My husband, Skip, had just asked me that day to look at his right calf. He said it had been aching and wondered if I could see anything. It hadn't felt warm, and I didn't see anything so we both thought it was just a muscle cramp. However, after hearing this report, I thought he should go see his doctor just in case.

That next day, Skip did go see his doctor. It ended up he had not one but two blood clots in his right calf. Had it not been for that news report, both of us would have continued assuming it was nothing more than a simple cramp. *"The Silent Killer"* got its name because often times DVT strikes with no symptoms or symptoms so mild that they are ignored. In Skip's case, he truly thought he just had a muscle cramp. The area wasn't red, hot or swollen.

The NBC journalist, David Bloom, was only 39 years old when he died from a pulmonary embolism believed to be brought on by a DVT while doing a job he loved – traveling with the 3rd Infantry Division in Iraq.

Skip's DVT hit, ironically, at the start of DVT awareness week. While, thankfully he is one of the lucky ones, though he does still live with one blood clot. He immediately started on blood thinners which he remains on today. One of the clots never dissolved so he is one of those cases that the clot is thought to be permanent, and he will have to take the blood thinners for the rest of his life. We are just grateful for the insistence of my angel to listen to that news report - grateful that he has the rest of his life to live.

The Sign

About six month ago I was driving along lost in thought. I was on my way to an exhibit that was about one hour from my home. It was about two months after my sister-in-laws death, and we were right in the middle of a lot of chaos. I was mulling over in my mind all of the things that still had to happen before her house sale deadline. I wondered why things had to happen the way they did and had the fleeting thought of how badly I missed my father who would always give me a good spiritual talking to. Not two minutes later I passed a street sign that said *"Victor Street"*. I smiled broadly, for I knew that was a sign that my dad was with me, as always. I felt suddenly peaceful.

John Edward

About six or eight months after my parent's deaths, I went to hear John Edward, the psychic medium, speak. It was in an auditorium in Cincinnati, Ohio, and I went along with my brother Lee and his wife, Dorothy. I desperately wanted to hear from my mom and dad, but it didn't happen. What did happen though, shortly after John began speaking, is he said their names in reference to something else. For some reason he said *Victor and Josephine.* When he said that, my heart skipped a beat. At the time, when I realized he wasn't talking to us, I thought it couldn't have been for us. But then later after reading his books, I realized that it was indeed a message that my parents were there. They didn't come through for us that day because someone else needed it more. But the chances of John saying *Victor & Josephine?* An *Angelwhisper!*

(The following story is from my brother, Lee)

Olivia

My tenth grandchild, Olivia, was born a month before Dad died. Dad never got to see her. One morning, shortly before Dad died, my sister talked to Mom. Mom said she had seen Dad during the night. When asked what he said, Mom said Dad had told her that he got to hold the baby.

I thought that was neat, so I related the story to my daughter, Cherie. She told me the same morning, she asked her older daughter, Ellie (who was 3 1/2 at the time) whether she had any dreams during the night. Ellie said yes, Great Grandpa was there and he held Olivia.

Cherie asked what Great Grandpa said, and Ellie replied

"he said to take good care of my baby." She then added, "I told him that was my baby not his baby!" Great Grandpa just laughed.

Coincidence? I don't think so.

Grandson Visit

"...I am 81 years old and have had a lot of experiences with the angels. Most recently my grandson came into our house and visited – wanted to apologize for not being at home when we left to go south. Said he wanted to say 'good bye'. When we got home down south, we got a phone call from his parents and he had died 3 days before he came to visit me..."

L.D.
South Dakota

I Still Remember My Angel...

"...After not being able to speak and my right arm being useless, the doctor cut two holes in my head and drained blood off my brain. I have two stainless plates. After recovery at home... I rolled over on my right side. The angel was standing at the side of my bed. She was about 30-35 years old and very beautiful with deep dimples and long hair which covered about half of her ears and down her back. She was dressed in a robe. Her face and robe were a beige color. She never spoke just stood there with a big smile for about five minutes, then faded away very slowly. The next morning I couldn't hardly explain it to my wife I was still so overcome. I am 92 1/2 years old now, and my wife is in heaven. But you know I can still see this beautiful angel just like it was this morning. I know she was telling me I would be ok..."

J.K.

San Luis Obispo, CA

Angel Assistance

"I very much believe in angels. In 1996 I went over 140 ft. cliff as a passenger in a hatchback car. April 20, 1996 returning from Cal Neva Casino to Incline Village, my girlfriend was driving and we had left our husbands at the townhouse having a drink, when I realized she was drunk. I thought of calling my husband, but since he was having a drink and he was in his 80's, I did not call. She could not turn the lights on, and all the cars kept flashing their lights at us. I kept telling her to pull over. She was going about 50, and the road suddenly turned to the left and she went straight ahead. It took an eternity to come down 140 ft, especially since the car was small. The paramedics were directly behind us. He told me we were airborne before dropping down and could not understand how we did not roll down the hill (which would have killed us), but also that when we landed we did not hit a tree even though the car kept going between the trees, and one tree trunk went through the back door about 20 inches from where I was sitting. Just when I was wondering how we were going to get help, my door was pried open. A young boy, 14, named John said: 'Help is on its way, you are going to be alright'. He kept kissing my hand and reassuring me. His eyes were dark blue like sky on a clear day, and his hair was strawberry blond. A couple of ringlets had formed close to his face, and I knew at once he was an angel. He took his sweater off and stood in that cold with nothing but a tank top undershirt till the paramedics arrived. I had a compressed fracture and had to be taken to the hospital. I never saw him again. I kept asking if any paramedics had a son with that description, no one did!"

E.L.
Brentwood, CA

Dedicated to Joshua

"...11 years ago, God blessed us with an 'earth-bound angel'. He was almost 17 years old, spastic quadriplegic, blind, non-verbal, seizure disorder, 65 pounds, skin and bones with open bed sores - the most severe stage of cerebral palsy. I had just started work with individuals with cerebral palsy. I was scared to death. He was soooo medically fragile. As time went by, fear turned to love. I prayed God would let me take him home. I lived in an all-male environment. God answered my prayer. He is now 27, we understand his body language. He weighs at least 125 lbs, (feeds through a G-tube) He outlived his expectancy. Love, God and Angels work miracles. When he goes to bed at night, I always tell him to sleep 'with the angels'. Recently God took another angel home, my son of 26 years..."

C.W.
Arkansas

Little Sister

My "little sister" succumbed to Anorexia Nervosa on July 25, 2009 at the young age of 31. She battled her eating disorder in secret for 8-9 years. She left numerous journals of her thoughts and food intake which are a physical proof of her lost and tormented soul. In the summer months after her passing I started to have suicidal thoughts. On September 9, 2009 between 3-4AM, I went outside after reading about grief and heaven. I sat on the patio and spoke to my sister as I watched the full moon in the night sky. There were a few clouds surrounding this beautiful moon. As I watched, two clouds grew nearer to the moon and slowly formed two long angel wings with two stars shifting above the wings. I was filled with such a feeling of happiness. I knew for sure that my sister was giving me a sign that she loved me. I knew she was at peace and that gave me a reason to live ...

M.V.
Strabane, PA

Angel Nudge

I've had some experiences that I believe angels had a hand in. I used to work day shift and my husband, Don, worked afternoons. After work Don would go and play pool and return home very late. One night I heard a prowler outside my bedroom window. I was very scared. I prayed for Don to come home. He got home shortly afterward asking "What is wrong?" I told him there was a prowler outside. We went outside and the prowler ran off. I asked Don what made him come home so early. He said a feeling came over him of concern. I believe!

C.C
Tampa, FL

Chapter 7:

Angel Stories & Quotes

Remember to welcome strangers in your homes. There were some who did that and welcomed angels without knowing it.[67]

Angels mean messengers and ministers. Their function is to execute the plan of divine providence, even in earthly things.[68]

"...I think that we all have Angel stories. As I have always believed in Angels, this book enlightened my thoughts and a review of happenings in the past. I fully realize that I had to have had help in some of the things that confronted me. Best Wishes."

B.B.
Abilene, TX

"I have been a believer of angels for 80 years."

J.S.
St Louis, MO

---

67   *The Holy Bible*, Hebrews 13:2.
68   *Quote*, St Thomas Aquinas.

Angel Light

Excerpt from my journal/March 2001

…Mom has been talking a lot about dad and said he was going to be coming for her soon. This morning she kept talking about dad having been there. She said he was in the bedroom and came in to see her from outside, through the windows. She said he was surrounded by real white light. I didn't doubt this, in fact I believed she was seeing a lot of him.

Then a few days later, I was getting ready to go into mom's apartment from the hallway. One of mom's neighbors saw me and stopped me. She asked if that was Josephine's apartment, and I answered her that it was. She told me that a few nights ago she had seen a very bright light coming out of the window of my mother's apartment, and it had scared her. She walked away from me then, still looking nervous and a bit frightened. I stood rooted to the spot, remembering what mom had told me about seeing my dad – and the light…

I'm Here

About a year after my parent's death, I had all my kids over for dinner on Sunday afternoon. I made homemade gnocchi, which was a favorite dish of my dad's. Just as we had gathered around the table and finished saying grace something strange happened. A shot glass that I had bought my dad when we had toured the Zane Grey museum together suddenly flew off the shelf. It didn't just fall off, it shot off with great speed, yet didn't break. Only my youngest son and I witnessed it. Everyone else only heard it as it fell. My son and I looked at each other and smiled. We both knew dad was there and blessed the fact that we were all together...

Angels at Work

One Friday afternoon my husband, Skip, and I were headed west on I-80 planning to meet friends in Michigan City. It started to rain as the sky darkened. It rained harder as the wind picked up speed. Suddenly, Skip abruptly pulled the wheel to the right and pulled the car under the protection of a bridge and skidded to a stop. Just then, with no warning, what appeared to be a funnel cloud passed directly in front of the bridge. We were rocked in the car as the winds and hail pummeled us. Cars pulled in behind us. When the worst of it seemed past, we continued on but we soon found that there was something amiss with the car and we were forced to turn around, head for home and cancel the trip. We found out later that there were many accidents ahead of us on the stretch of roadway leading to Michigan City. Skip couldn't explain what it was that made him abruptly turn the wheel as he did. Nor could the mechanic find anything wrong with our car. I'd say our guardian angels were at work.

There is a poem by Linda Ellis called *The Dash*. In it she talks about the dates of birth and death as recorded on a tombstone with just a little dash in the middle. We need to realize *the dash* is our life! How are you spending your dash?

Special Quotes

It is very important to pray for others, because when you pray for someone, an angel goes and sits on the shoulder of that person.[69]

And do not forget to entertain strangers, for thereby some have entertained angels unawares.[70]

Everyone, no matter how humble he may be, has angels to watch over him…They have been given the task of keeping watch over you…You will spend a happy eternity with the angels, get to know them here.[71]

God has a plan for each of us, and what we want and ask for, may not fit into that plan.[72]

Do not compare yourself to others. You have a unique destiny and mission that only you can accomplish.[73]

---

69 *Quote,* The Virgin Mary to the children at Medjugorje.
70 *The Holy Bible,* Hebrew 13:2.
71 *Quote,* Pope Piux XII in an address to a group of Americans a few days before his death in 1958.
72 *Quote,* Albert Einstein.
73 *Quote,* Mariane Pearl, Author, Wife of Journalist Daniel Pearl. *We Empower,* Maria Shriver 2008 California Governor and First Lady's Conference on Women, New York, NY.

Don't listen to experts if your gut tells you something is wrong with their advice.[74]

Keep your honor.[75]

Aim High, focus your energies, and color everything you do with a sense of urgency.[76]

Feed and follow your passion. As you work to find it, you should know that sometimes, your passion just finds you.[77]

Make an issue of everything that will make your children better adults: let everything else go.[78]

You must do the thing you think you cannot do.[79]

---

74 *Quote,* Mary Tillman, Author, Boots on the Ground By Dusk: My Tribute to Pat Tillman. *We Empower,* Maria Shriver 2008 California Governor and First Lady's Conference on Women, New York, NY.

75 *Quote,* Tim Russert, Former Moderator, Meet The Press, Women's Conference, 2006. *We Empower,* Maria Shriver 2008 California Governor and First Lady's Conference on Women, New York, NY.

76 *Quote,* Michael J Fox, Actor, Author & Founder of /the Michael J. Fox Foundation for Parkinson's Research. *We Empower,* Maria Shriver 2008 California Governor and First Lady's Conference on Women, New York, NY.

77 *Quote,* Condoleeza Rice, United States Secretary of State. *We Empower,* Maria Shriver 2008 California Governor and First Lady's Conference on Women, New York, NY.

78 *Quote,* Elizabeth Edwards, Author, Saving Graces. *We Empower,* Maria Shriver 2008 California Governor and First Lady's Conference on Women, New York, NY.

79 *Quote,* Eleanor Roosevelt.

True life is lived when tiny changes occur.[80]

One can never pay in gratitude; one can only pay "in kind" somewhere else in life.[81]

Go confidently in the direction of your dreams! Live the life you've imagined. As you simplify your life, the laws of the universe will be simpler.[82]

It is good to have an end to journey towards, but it is the journey that matters in the end.[83]

We are all on different paths. Wherever you find yourself in your journey, I hope this book has been helpful to you. On the next pages are some music and books that I find inspiring, so I have included them here. Perhaps you will like them too, and I hope they help you. I welcome your suggestions. As always, I wish you the best life has to offer.

Marcy

---

80 *Quote,* Leo Tolstoy. *Prayers to the Great Creator: Prayers & Declarations for a Meaningful Life,* Julia Cameron 1997, 1998, 1999, 2008 Julia Cameron. Published by the Penguin Group, New York, NY.

81 *Quote,* Anne Morrow Lindbergh. *Each Day a New Beginning, Daily Meditations for Women,* 1982 by the Hazelden Foundation, Harper & Row Publishers, New York, NY.

82 *Quote,* Henry David Thoreau. *Prayers to the Great Creator: Prayers & Declarations for a Meaningful Life,* Julia Cameron 1997, 1998, 1999, 2008 Julia Cameron. Published by the Penguin Group, New York, NY.

83 *Quote,* Ursula K. LeGuin. *The Circle: How the Power of a Single Wish Can Change Your Life, Laura Day,* 2001 by Laura Day. Published by the Penguin Group, New York, NY.

Recommended Music:
To Where You Are, Josh Groban
I Hope You Dance, Lee Ann Womack
You Raise Me Up, Josh Groban
<u>Anything</u> by Andrea Bocelli

Recommended Reading:
The Shack, William Paul Young
Anything by Dr. Wayne W. Dyer especially *The Power of Intention*
Simple Abundance, A Daybook of Comfort and Joy, Sarah Ban Breathnach
For One More Day, Mitch Albom
The Last Lecture, Randy Pausch
90 Minutes in Heaven, Don Piper
Heaven is Real, Don Piper
Daily Devotions Inspired by 90 Minutes in Heaven, Don Piper & Cecil Murphey
ANY books by John Edward
Knit Together: Discover God's Pattern For Your Life, Debbie Macomber
When God Winks, Squire Rushnell
When God Winks at You, Square Rashnell
The Five People You Meet in Heaven, Mitch Albom
The Alchemist, Paulo Coelho
The Circle: How the Power of a Single Wish Can Change Your Life, Laura Day
Life's Golden Ticket, Brendon Burchard
The Power of Now, Eckhart Tolle
Changing Your Course: The 5-Step Guide to getting the Life You Want, Bob & Melinda Blanchard
We Are Their Heaven, Allison DuBois
Don't Kiss Them Goodbye, Allison DuBois

Secrets of the Monarch, Allison DuBois

The Death and Life of Charlie St Cloud, Ben Sherwood

The Christmas Shoes, Donna Van Liere

Finding Noel, Richard Paul Evans

Touched By An Angel, Martha Williamson (This hit television series starring Della Reese, Roma Downey and John Dye was full of inspirational and real angelic experiences)

How We Grieve, Thomas Attig

Life After Loss, Bot Deits

I Don't Know What to Say, Dr Robert Buckman

A Gift of Hope – How We Survive Our Tragedies, Robert Veninga

The Art of Racing in the Rain, Garth Stein

The Travelers Gift, Andy Andrews

The Noticer, Andy Andrews

Live What You Love, Bob & Melinda Blanchard

The Walk Series: The Walk, Miles to Go, The Road to Grace, A Step of Faith, Walking on Water, Richard Paul Evans

Heaven is for Real, Todd Burpo

You Were Born for This, Bruce Wilkinson

Eat, Pray, Love, Elizabeth Gilbert

Life Without Limits, Nick Vujicic

Resilience, Elizabeth Edwards

Thank You

Thank you so much for purchasing *"Angelwhispers: Listen for them in your life..."*.

If you have a angel story that you would like to share, or comments about this book, I would love to hear from you! If I can use it in a future edition, I will gladly send you a free copy of the new book.

My sincere thanks, and to you I extend my wishes for the best of everything.

Marcy

_____

_____

_____

_____

Please indicate (yes or no) whether I may use your name if I use your helpful advice:

YES, please give credit to _____

(Please print)

NO, please use my advice, but do not use my name in the book

(Either way, Yes or No, if I use your advice or personal experience, I'll send you a free copy of the new edition.)

Reorder Form

90-DAY MONEY-BACK GUARANTEE

❑ YES. Please rush _____ additional copies of *"Angelwhispers: Listen for them in your life..."* and my FREE copy of the bonus booklet *"Victor's Story"* for only $9.95 plus $3.98 postage & handling (Total of $13.93). I understand that I must be completely satisfied or can return it within 90 days for a full and prompt refund of my purchase price. The FREE gift is mine to keep regardless. *Want to save even more?* Do a favor for a relative or close friend and order a second book and shipping is FREE! That's 2 for only $20 postpaid.

Angelwhispers:
Listen for them in your life...

VISA   DISCOVER
MASTERCARD   AMEX

I am enclosing $_____ by: ❑ Check ❑ Money Order (Make checks payable to Shaw Creative)

Charge my credit card   Signature _____

Card No. _____   Exp. date _____

Name _____

Address _____

City _____   State _____   Zip _____

❑ Yes! I'd like to know about specials and new books as they become available. My email address is: _____

Mail To: **Shaw Creative • PO Box 703 • Uniontown, Ohio 44685**
http://www.maryanneshaw.com

Use this coupon to order *"Angelwhispers: Listen for them in your life..."* for a friend or family member -- or copy the ordering information onto a plain piece of paper and mail to:

Shaw Creative
PO Box 703
Uniontown, Ohio 44685

Valued Customer Reorder Form

Order this...	If you want a book on...	Cost...	Number of Copies...
NEW **Victor's Story: Till We Meet Again**	True story of Victor's amazing life that spanned 94 years. Filled with Victor's stories and anecdotes from his boyhood days in Waynesburg, Ohio through his adult life including his very special angel stories. The 7 Life Lessons through a daughter's eyes will inspire you to live the life you were meant to lead.	$12.95	
The 9 Week Miracle	True story of a son's survival after being burned 46% of his body in a freak accident. Its message of triumph over adversity leads to the discovery of the 7 Life Lessons we all need to overcome in our own headships. Join Nick *The 9 Week Miracle*. You'll never look at life the same way again.	$9.95	
Angelwhispers: *Listen for them in your life...*	The coincidences that happen in our lives, the little nudges in our minds... that is our angels! Learn to recognize the *Angelwhispers* in your daily life for joy, blessings and abundance.	$9.95	
Angel Stories from Across America	Angel encounters, stories, messages and accounts from readers all across the country. Sure to inspire you with its descriptions of hope and faith in action for everyday including the times of adversity we all face.	$9.95	
Amish Gardening Secrets	You too can learn the special gardening secrets the Amish use to produce huge tomato plants and bountiful harvests. Information packed 800-plus collection for you to tinker with and enjoy.	$9.95	
	Sub total		
	Postage & Handling (1 - 3 books) $3.98 **(4 or more books)** $4.98		
	TOTAL		

90-DAY MONEY-BACK GUARANTEE

Please rush me the items marked above. I understand that I must be completely satisfied or I can return any item within 90 days with proof of purchase for a full and prompt refund of my purchase price.

I am enclosing $_____ by: ❏ Check ❏ Money Order
(Make checks payable to Shaw Creative)

VISA *MasterCard* *DISCOVER* *AMEX*

Charge my credit card Signature _____

Card No. _____ Exp. Date _____

Name _____

Address _____

City _____ State _____ Zip _____

Telephone Number (_____) _____

❏ Yes! I'd like to know about specials and new books as they become available. My email address is: _____

Mail To: **Shaw Creative** • PO Box 703, • Uniontown, Ohio 44685
http://www.maryanneshaw.com

NEW

VICTOR'S STORY: *Till We Meet Again*

Victor knew that life's priorities should be God first, then family and then career and he lived this example every day. This heartwarming book will move you one minute and have you laughing out loud the next. Truly the story of an amazing life...

- -

THE 9 WEEK MIRACLE

A remarkable journey demonstrating the inherent goodness that exists in people, even perfect strangers. Their willingness to help bridge the gap between suffering and healing was evident in the *Amish garage-raising.* A remarkable event! It is a saga of faith, gritty determination and endurance.

- -

ANGELWHISPERS: *Listen for them in your life...*

Do you Believe in Angels? Angels are ready to help us in lots of ways. They can protect us from danger, reduce our fears, pain, worries and even help us find ways to cope with our problems. Learn the techniques in this book to improve every aspect of your life – *even your wealth!*

- -

ANGEL STORIES FROM ACROSS AMERICA

More words of hope and encouragement from the author of Angelwhispers: Listen for them in your life. This new book has true angel stories of encounters with loved ones from readers from all over the country!

- -

AMISH GARDENING SECRETS

There's something for everyone in *Amish Gardening Secrets.* This BIG collection contains over 800 gardening hints, suggestions, time savers and tonics that have been passed down over the years in Amish communities and elsewhere.

All these important books carry our NO-RISK GUARANTEE. Enjoy them for three full months. If you are not 100% satisfied simply return the book(s) along with proof of purchase, for a prompt, "no questions asked" refund!

http://www.maryanneshaw.com